An author can only hope and pray ⊥ [the way will be challenged to pick up the passion for the subject of their book and pursue it to deeper depths and broader scopes. Such a one has been raised up by God in the person of Susan Dewbrew. While studying my book dealing with God's plan for woman in one of her Christian Leadership University courses, and having already struggled for some time with this issue, God planted in her heart a deep passion to pursue the subject further.

As a result, Susan spent the last fifteen years in research regarding the gender issue. During this time she also laid her heart bare before the Lord seeking a deeper understanding of the Kingdom of God and learning that His Kingdom's solid foundation is love, which leaves no place for fleshly hierarchy of any kind. The results: *Unleashing the Kingdom*, Books 1-3. I have learned so much as I've read these books. Indeed, my student has become my teacher.

Susan hits hard (and I do mean hard) at the centuries of the subjugation of women, but she never once hints that retribution should be the antidote. Rather, she sets the example of gracious forgiveness grounded in love to those who have done the oppressing.

Susan's emphasis on the gospel of the Kingdom is the heart of her teaching in these books. This sometimes elicits the use of some big words and lots of referrals to the Greek and Hebrew. But now and then she inserts some of her humor, making one chuckle in the midst of some heavy point she is making. This gives the reader a peek into her personable, down-to-earth self who is a true lover of Jesus.

These three books that comprise *Unleashing the Kingdom* are each one a must-read for anyone desiring to understand the importance and power of equality for all in the Kingdom of God. In them, Susan also delves into the correct translation of Paul's very misunderstood writings, along with tips on how to hear the voice of God. All three volumes are a treasure trove for anyone with an open heart who is hungry for biblical truth that will deepen their walk with God.

— JOANNE KRUPP

AUTHOR OF *WOMAN, GOD'S PLAN NOT MAN'S TRADITION*

I love this series! I love the spirit of it. And I love the revelation truths it has for all of us. Thank you, Susan, for your faithful obedience to both the Word and the Spirit which has produced this incredible gift to the Body of Christ. Thank you, Steve, for putting this gift into such beautiful language.

Twenty years ago, the Lord began to take Susan on a journey revealing His heart for His Bride. Our paths intersected when she enrolled in distance learning classes with our online school, Christian Leadership University. As a graduate student, Susan excelled in her work, and we posted two of her final course papers on our website to be a blessing and resource to others. It is thrilling to see how the Lord used her studies with CLU as a stepping-stone on her journey. We are excited and grateful to God to see the incredible fruit and ministry being born through her life!

With refreshing optimism and not a hint of the feminist Jezebel spirit, Susan invites us to travel with her as she discovers more of God's plan for women, His Church and indeed, the world. In what could potentially be a divisive presentation, Susan's sweet spirit and sincere humility make her message easy to receive, as does her passionate love for Christ and His Church, which comes shining through on every page.

And please note: this is not simply a series about the "women's issues." As important as they are, there is more here than that. The Lord has given Susan a two-fold revelation, which also includes key insights on what it means to be a "king and priest" ruling and reigning with Christ. Her perspective on Kingdom living, what that looks like, and how we should every day bring heaven to earth, is equally powerful. I wholeheartedly agree with this message. The Kingdom of heaven is not a far-off place. As we release Christ and His life and power through our lives in supernatural ways, miracles manifest and *it is done* here on earth as it is in heaven!

Susan is careful to never once let this pure message devolve into male bashing or any spirit of criticism or condemnation. Instead, Susan rightfully declares, "Unity is the key to power, and honor is the key to unity." Indeed, God has been emphasizing 1 Peter 2:17 (NASB) to my heart over and over: we are to "honor all people." *All* people, all mankind, everyone—including women. Susan's teaching on honoring one another's differences (as man and woman) resonates with me because the Lord has been teaching me this as well. To be sure, this message is timely for us all.

Please read these important books with an open mind and most of all with an open heart. Let the Holy Spirit reveal all the Truth He has to share with you on this crucial subject. You will learn things you have never known before. You will come away with a fresh understanding of familiar Scriptures. You will find peace from the tension and questions you've had about women in ministry and leadership. You will be blessed!

— **MARK VIRKLER**

PRESIDENT, CHRISTIAN LEADERSHIP UNIVERSITY

WWW.CLUONLINE.COM

AUTHOR OF OVER 50 BOOKS INCLUDING

4 KEYS TO HEARING GOD'S VOICE AND

OVERFLOW OF THE SPIRIT

Susan Dewbrew has allowed the Holy Spirit to use her passion for people to write a three-part series of books that points the reader toward the liberating quality of unity. In this work, *Unleashing the*

Kingdom, Susan methodically walks you through a well-ordered path of right behavior that can lead you to peace and tranquil living, God's way. She skillfully uses the Holy Scriptures to help the reader understand the tragedy of division and the triumph of God-ordained unity. This is a series of writings that can be used with Bible study groups or individual periods of devotion. You cannot go wrong with this God-inspired work. I offer my most enthusiastic endorsement for *Unleashing the Kingdom*.

— REVEREND DR. MICHAEL A. EVANS, SR.

SENIOR PASTOR

BETHLEHEM BAPTIST CHURCH, MANSFIELD, TX

SUSAN DEWBREW

with STEVE PIXLER

UNLEASHING
THE
KINGDOM

TAKING DOMINION THROUGH
THE UNITY OF MEN AND WOMEN

THE WOMAN'S PLACE

UNLEASHING THE KINGDOM

TAKING DOMINION THROUGH THE UNITY OF MEN AND WOMEN

THE WOMAN'S PLACE

SUSAN DEWBREW

WITH STEVE PIXLER

KINGDOM BREWING | MANSFIELD, TX

CREATING & CURATING KINGDOM RESOURCES

UNLEASHING THE KINGDOM: THE WOMAN'S PLACE (BOOK 1)

As a matter of honor, this work deliberately capitalizes pronouns referring to the Father, Son, and Holy Spirit. Conversely, the name of satan or any related names or pronouns are intentionally not capitalized.

CONTENTS

FOREWORD

STEVE PIXLER

This book series changed my life. I worked on this project as Susan's ghostwriter—a Holy-Ghost-writer, I've jokingly said!—which is why my name is on the cover. But I was first introduced to Susan's work on women's issues when she and Gregory, her husband and my dear friend, visited our church and shared with me a copy of a small, previous work Susan had published on the topic. Since I am a pastor and writer, people often give me their books to read, and I always flip through the pages dutifully, honoring the time and effort people put into their works. Sometimes a work stands out as special. That's what I sensed immediately with Susan's work. It was unusually special. I read it straight through that afternoon after church.

Throughout the years, I had read countless books on the women's issue, and I was immediately impressed with Susan's clarity, warm style and strong passion that reverberated through every page. But the thing that really captured my attention—that made me sit up with a startled, "Hello!"—was the fact that Susan had really done her homework. As a pastor, amateur theologian and ardent student of Scripture, I pay close attention to how people handle the Word. As I mentioned, I had read volumes of material on the question of women in ministry, and I felt like I had considered the issue from just about every angle. Yet here was Susan, opening up new ways of seeing the Scriptures, and it immediately fascinated me.

Let me give you a little bit of background. I was raised in a super-conservative Pentecostal denomination. As you may know, Pentecostals tend to be an eclectic group, and our corner of the Pentecostal church world was no different. There were all sorts who gathered around the freedom of worship and expression that Pentecostals encouraged, and that freedom to be a bit weird meant that unusual doctrines blew through like March winds.

The question of women in ministry was no different. There were all sorts of opinions and explanations bandied about all my young life. My grandfather and father, both pastors in Fort Worth, TX, disagreed sharply on women in ministry. My grandfather was all for letting women preach, pastor and do anything the men could do. My father, strongly influenced by my mother's childhood pastor, believed that the Scriptures plainly told the women to be silent, though dad was sure that only applied to formal teaching and preaching. Nothing made dad more indignant than being told that he either had to let women preach or make them be totally silent—as in, no singing, amen-ing or teaching Sunday School. Dad would just grunt in disgust at that comeback.

I remember growing up hearing my dad and "Pappy," as I called my grandfather, fuss about "women preachers" for hours on long road trips to regional camp-meetings all over the South. My dad was sure that Paul simply nixed the idea of women in the pulpit, but Pappy was sure that Paul only said women couldn't "usurp authority," as the King James Version put it. "If the pastor lets her preach, James, then she's not usurping authority!" Pappy would protest, his tenor voice rising to the highest register. With my dad all the time shaking his head in stubborn disagreement. "Ain't what it said! Ain't what it said!" And on and on they went, fussing the hours away. My mischievous ten-year-old self loved every minute of it.

When I became a pastor, I embraced my dad's conviction that women are not allowed by Scripture to teach men. They can sing, teach children, be used in the gifts of the Spirit (including prophecy), but they cannot exercise the formal authority of ruling over men from the official seat of judgment, which was the pulpit, as we saw it. I believed it, not just because my dad did, but because I felt like he was right in what he concluded Paul meant. When Paul said that he did not permit women to teach or exercise authority over men, he meant exactly that. And to acquiesce to modern sensibilities just to avoid being considered misogynistic looked like cowardice to me.

After many years of serving as a pastor, my views slowly but surely began to shift. I started taking seriously the varied objections to my settled point of view. I had started shifting on so many legalistic traditions I'd inherited that movement on the women's issue wasn't so much of a leap anymore. But change did prove to be difficult. The first time I invited a women to teach at our church, my father walked out in protest. It was dramatic, people! Though we got everything sorted out between us later, my dad went to his grave believing that I was compromising significant truths that would undermine biblical doctrine. These days, I am comforted by the fact that he is in the presence of the Lord and sees clearly how wrong we all were for so long.

By the time I met Susan and Gregory, I had fully embraced the biblical and spiritual freedom women have to minster alongside men. No doubt, that's what Gregory was "feeling out" when he handed me her book. I later learned that Susan had encountered fierce resistance from many churches and pastors, and they were nervous how I would respond as they visited and considered attending our church. Good thing we met when we did! A few years earlier would have been a different story altogether. Thank God for divine timing.

Regardless, as I have gotten to know Susan, I have been blown away by her honesty and integrity when handling Scripture. Over and over, as we've worked through writing these three books, Susan has insisted on doing more of that careful homework that first drew me into her perspective on the women's issue. I love the fact that she refuses to settle for an inferior explanation that sounds right but isn't. That's what Paul calls "plausible arguments" in Colossians 2:4 (ESV), and Susan flatly refuses to wield them. She will do the work necessary to get what Paul actually said exactly right. And that still makes me sit up and go, "Hello!" with pleasant surprise. I love it.

I think you will too.

One more thing. I am fully committed to the message espoused by this book of unleashing the Kingdom through the unity of men and women. In fact, I am even more committed now after working through each word, each line, each page. I approached this project with curiosity. I have always been eager to learn more about this subject. But through the time we've worked together, I've developed a deeper passion—even a sense of divine mandate!—than I've ever had for this issue. I truly believe that Susan is spot on when she declares that the Kingdom of God cannot fully come in the world as long as the female half of the Church is silenced. The coming of Christ's Kingdom in the right-now, real world is my life-message, so I didn't need much urging to buy into that. The Kingdom message is my sweet spot. But understanding the role of women in advancing the Kingdom and accepting the mandate to advocate for that outcome is a new thing since beginning this project with Susan. As I said, this book series has changed my life. There is a new anointing on my life since reading this book, and I believe the same will happen for you.

Susan and Gregory now attend our church and serve on our Lead Team as Team Leads for our Prayer & Prophetic Team. I've now had the opportunity to work in partnership with them in so many different situations. These people are the real deal, and I fully and highly recommend Susan's work to you. Dive in. Read slow. Back up and read it again. Marinate long in every phrase. Nothing here is wasted. Even portions of the series that seem like we're taking the long way 'round the world are deliberately and prayerfully included to release every layer of revelation that Holy Spirit has graciously commissioned Susan to share with you. Most of all, as you read may "His Kingdom come, His will be done on earth as it is in heaven."

READ ME FIRST!

The human race is divided. And that division begins within the relationship that brings humans into being—the relationship between men and women. Actually, the division starts one level deeper in the breach sin caused between God and people. But in terms of human relationships and the division that plagues the planet, the breakdown between people begins with the breakdown between mom and dad. We learn division at home.

Every human is conceived in a moment of physical oneness that rarely manifests spiritually beyond the bedroom. Even the best of male and female relations are fractured due to sin, and those fractures work out into human interactions across the social spectrum. As kids grow up, the divide that lies at the heart of fallen families creeps out as suspicion toward neighbors, playmates, kids at school, coworkers and political opponents. The fissures widen into outright hostility, and human relations deteriorate into racism, sexism, ageism, classism, nationalism—and all the other "isms" that force people into warring factions.

This is *the* primary strategy of the enemy. All other demonic strategies flow from this one: "divide and conquer." And because all human division flows from the male-female divide, satan works super-hard to stoke the flames of pride and resentment that foster fear-driven supremacy and subjugation. I am not exaggerating when I say that the division between men and women is the number one item on hell's agenda.

The kingdom of darkness wields global power by exploiting human division, which means that satan must keep men and women snarling at each other's throats in order to keep the pipeline of hate flowing. By "familiating" (to make up a word!) male insecurity and female resentment, the enemy seeks to ensure that every human grows up in a toxic environment of tense competition.

And that idea—that male and female conflict lies at the heart of all human division—is the central idea of this book series. Well, at least it is *half* of the central idea. The other half is that Jesus came to heal human division. He came to bring reconciliation between God and people that would reverse the curse of human division and release shalom into the world—God's peace that heals fractured hearts and makes people whole. Jesus came to release heaven into earth, to *unleash His Kingdom* and to transform human society.

It is my deepest conviction that Jesus unleashes the Kingdom by healing the rift between men and women. Thus, the Kingdom cannot be fully unleashed as long as men and women remain divided. The Kingdom of God brings healing to the nations, but it begins at home. Better yet, healing begins in the heart, and the transformed heart transforms the home. The transformed home transforms all of human society, for all societal relations are shaped by our *family of origin*.

The curse of sin fell directly on the first male and female on the planet, and when Jesus came to break the curse, He went right to the heart of the matter. The heart of the matter is the *heart*. By reconciling people to God through the cross of Jesus, by regenerating humans through the new birth, by reforming families through saved mom and dads and by reconstituting His Church around these newly healed relations, Jesus releases a new way of being human into all human relations.

Young children who grow up in this kind of Kingdom shalom carry healing with them wherever they go. They become world-changers. Jesus is literally changing the world one person at a time. One person at a time becomes one marriage, one family, one church, one city, one nation at a time.

> *The Kingdom is unleashed when men and women are united. Yet the greatest challenge to male-female unity is male-female equality.*

The Kingdom is unleashed when men and women are united. Yet the greatest challenge to male-female unity is male-female equality. As long as men are viewed as superior and women as inferior, true unity is impossible. Men and women can form uneasy alliances, even work together to do loads of good in the world. But the true creational, covenantal unity that reveals the image of God and achieves God-honoring, God-revealing dominion over the earth cannot come as long as one gender dominates the other.

Male supremacy has dominated human society since the Fall of humankind in the Garden of Eden. As Father God mournfully predicted,

> *To the woman He said, "I will greatly multiply your pain in childbirth, in pain you will bring forth children; yet your desire will be for your husband, and he will rule over you." (Genesis 3:16)*

The inevitable consequence of sin, which humans chose, not God, was conflict between men and women. And this is exactly the same curse that Jesus died to break.

I want you to see this, for this is the foundation of everything we will talk about in this series: *conflict between men and women lies at the heart of all the conflict in the world.* Do you see that? The roots of the curse go back to the relationship between men and women, between parents and children, between God and people. It is silly to say that Jesus saves us from sin and heals our relationship with God, but then leaves us fighting with one another for supremacy. Not at all! The curse came upon male-female relations, and Jesus' death broke that curse *exactly where it started!* Jesus came to heal male-female relations. Is it any wonder that His first miracle was at a wedding?

Now, it will take me a while to prove my point. Three-books-in-a-series-worth of a "while," in fact. (Indeed this entire series just scratches the surface.) The reason it will take some time to prove my point is that we have to sift carefully like archeologists through layers of mindsets and worldviews that have been shaped by millennia of curse-driven concepts. Strata after strata of long-held beliefs that are so deeply grounded in our hearts that we don't even know that it is a "belief"—we just see it as reality.

The saddest part of all is that the greatest obstacle to gender equality is actually the Church. Not the world —the Church. Or, to put it more exactly, the greatest obstacle to equality is the teachings of the Church that are shaped by cursed culture. We have pietized and religion-ized the awful gender wars pronounced upon man and woman as the inevitable consequence of sin and made them the "Christian" norm.

How did we do this? By misinterpreting and misapplying Scripture. By allowing mindsets imported from the world to shape how we read and teach the Bible. Which means that the only way we can restore creational, covenantal equality to the world is to restore it to the Church, and that can only be done by revisiting and reinterpreting Scripture properly. That will take time. But our commitment to the inspiration and infallibility of Scripture means that we cannot take shortcuts with God's Word. We must take the time to get it right.

Oddly enough, it is an honest commitment to Scripture that causes part of the confusion. As we shall see, those who teach that women cannot lead in the Church base their conclusions on what appears to be a plain reading of Paul's teaching. Since they believe that they must honor the Word of God—and rightly so!—they advocate the subjugation of women. Many even do so reluctantly. They have no desire to trample women. Or anyone, for that matter.

Many "traditionalists" rightly discern that God's heart beats for the liberation of all suppressed people, especially women, so they celebrate the freedom of women in every way they possibly can in good conscience. But they simply cannot betray what they believe to be true. Honest students of Scripture cannot just dismiss passages that seem to relegate women to a lower status and prohibit them from leadership. There's no doubt that many passages seem to suggest just that.

> *The Kingdom brings transformation to the real world where we live, work and play.*

Pastors and leaders all over the world are working tirelessly to impact their communities with the Kingdom of God, and many have come to understand that the coming of the Kingdom restructures human society. The Kingdom ends slavery. The Kingdom ends economic oppression. The Kingdom ends the exploitation of children. The Kingdom brings transformation to the real world where we live, work and play.

And the pastors and leaders who get this also understand that the Kingdom of God breaks off the yoke of oppression from generations of abused, disempowered and exploited women. Many of them have been praying for years for innovative, Spirit-led ways to support and promote women. But some—to put it bluntly—are not sure what to think about it all. Some are torn between what their heart says is true and what their head believes the Bible says. It is a colossal conundrum, to say the least.

It's time to beat a new rhythm on that conundrum.

So what to do? They feel they must either violate God's heart or violate God's word—an impossible choice. And I feel their pain. I slogged through the same quagmire on my journey. (I'll tell you all about it later on.) But I have good news! There is no conflict between God's nature and God's Word. We don't have to choose between Scripture and equality for women. It's not an "either-or." Scripture actually *does not* teach the subordination of women. That idea comes from another kingdom, not from the Kingdom of God.

Christian leaders who have the courage to celebrate their wives, daughters and female friends becoming all God created them to be will *love* the revelations emerging from these chapters because they instinctively know that chauvinism and discrimination violate the *heart* of God. They know that making one group of people "less than" is *not* Christlike. These conflicted, heart-torn pastors and leaders are about to get their prayers answered.

I need to ask you a personal question. *How does this make you feel?* (How you *feel* will control what you receive as you read.)

Think about it for a moment.

Take your emotional pulse.

Does the idea of women in power make you excited or nervous? What do you think when you read statements like "women in authority" or "women in power"? What images come to mind? Do you shudder from the thought of a woman in charge? Did the bottom of your stomach tighten up just a bit?

If so, is it because your dominant perception of women is the Jezebel-type of over-controlling, manipulative female? Or was it because the Bible teaches that women should not have authority over men and therefore should not be in power? Are you fearful of a book that espouses equality for women? Does it sound like "feminism" in the church? Does it sound like heresy or biblical error?

It is important to assess how you feel. If your heart is closed due to fear, it will be almost impossible for Holy Spirit to shift your mind. My prayer is that you will open your heart. Even if it gets uncomfortable for a bit, hang in there.

Trust me, I know how you feel. I have struggled through all the uncertainties and questions that arise with such a daunting subject. I get it. Still, I invite you to take this journey with me. Take a deep breath and relax a bit. I promise it will be worth the trip. And, by the way, I promise what you learn will be biblically sound. I have no desire to embrace unbiblical ideas either. We all want God's truth. Nothing else.

So in our time together over the next three volumes, we will work our way through every significant passage that has been twisted to perpetuate the distortion of gender relations that occurred in the Fall. We will look at:

- 1 Corinthians 14, the "shush your women!" passage
- 1 Corinthians 11, the "headship" passage
- 1 Timothy 2 & 3, the "we don't permit women to teach" and "only men can be elders" passages
- Ephesians 5, the "wives must be subject to their husbands" passage
- Genesis 1 & 2, the "helper" passages

And more.

As we work our way through these passages, I will tell you my story. I will share how Holy Spirit led me through my own personal journey from being a "traditionalist," one who believed that Scripture restricted women from leading or teaching men, to one who came to believe that women are equal to men and can thus teach and lead men without restriction. And I came to believe this *through* Scripture—*because of Scripture!*—not in spite of it.

But throughout each book, we will do so much more than just work through the Scripture passages and tell my story. That will be fun all by itself, but the underlying message of the Kingdom of God will be the glue that binds the pages together. This series is not just about the liberation of women. It is about the liberation of the entire creation through the unleashing of the

Kingdom. The gospel of the Kingdom is the overarching theme that will enliven every personal experience and every Scripture interpretation.

Here's how we will approach the series.

- In Book 1, we will set the table. I'll share my personal experience with my journey from the traditional view of "The Woman's Place" to where I currently stand. And I will get started with some of the biblical passages that need to be addressed —specifically, 1 Corinthians 14 and the "shush your women!" passage.

- Then, we will wrap up Book 1 with a quick segue into the gospel of the Kingdom and get ready for Book 2, where the "Clash of Kingdoms" will be front and center. We will take the time in Book 2 to make sure that the Kingdom message penetrates down to the cellular level in our hearts.

- Finally, in Book 3, we will dig deep into the "proof texts" that are used and misused to ban women from leadership in the Church and in the world. We will talk about "Lies That Bind" and false filters that distort how we see Scripture.

As you might expect, all three books are essential to the overall message of *Unleashing the Kingdom*. Each book can be read as a free-standing volume. But in order to get the big picture, it's best to read all three in full and in order. We developed the volumes as a trilogy to make them more "digestible," rather than publishing one, intimidating monster manuscript. Hope that helps!

One final thing before we start. This series is not only about women's liberation—this is a series about human liberation. And human liberation is the liberation of both men and women released as the image of God working together in unity. Ironically, men are subjugated by the subjugation of women. Just as enslaving others is its own form of slavery—sometimes the slave is more free than the master—so male superiority is its own form of inferiority. Men who are truly free have no need to dominate anyone. Male domination, then, is an open admission of male insecurity. Raw power is always rooted in fear.

> **We cannot be fully who we were meant to be without healthy alignment with others.**

Moreover, God made men and women to be fully alive through union. In other words, men cannot be fully *men* without women. That doesn't mean that every man must be married; but it does mean that men must be properly aligned to women as a gender in order to be fully who God created men to be.

We are all social creatures by design. We cannot be fully who we were meant to be without healthy alignment with others. The hammer is useless without the nail. The glove has no purpose without the hand. The instrument has no melody without the musician. On and on—examples of essential union abound. The point is clear: God made men and women for union, and when one oppresses the other, both suffer.

So this series is not just about liberating women. It is about liberating *everyone*. It is about helping humans find the purpose for which God made us all. It is about unleashing the Kingdom in the world so that salvation may come to the nations. And the Kingdom cannot be unleashed as long as half of its citizens are subjugated.

But here I am getting ahead of myself and telling you all I need to tell you over three volumes. Let me stop here and invite you to take a journey with me. A journey that will empower both men and women, break the demonic division that grips our world and unleash the Kingdom of God in every nation under heaven. Sound ambitious? It is. But it is an ambition worth pursuing.

Ready?

Let's get started.

UNLEASHING THE KINGDOM (BOOK 1)

THE WOMAN'S PLACE

CHAPTER 1

MIXED SIGNALS

Every journey starts at a crossroads. Just the simple act of backing out of a driveway immediately presents options: shall we turn to the left or to the right? Shall we proceed north or south? East or west? Or shall we just cut diagonally across the lawn next door?

Hopefully, we make the right call and save the neighbor's fescue.

Cross-country driving notwithstanding, every journey leads to choices. Mine certainly did. My path to understanding the equality of women within the Kingdom of God started as a series of seemingly "fortuitous" turns that, in retrospect, were divinely directed. But I didn't know at the time that anything—or Anyone!—was directing my steps.

Thankfully, He was.

My journey of a thousand miles began at the crossroads of creation and culture, at the intersection where "how God made me" and "what the world wanted me to be" presented two quite different options. My journey started with "mixed signals."

Maybe you can relate.

Two Powerful Urges

There are two powerful urges driving every decision humans make: *creation* and *culture*. As I am using the terms here, *creation* is "how God made us," and *culture* is "what the world wants us to be." Some call it *nature* and *nurture*. I like *creation* and *culture* because it highlights "God" and "people" as two opposing forces that pull on us.

On the one hand, we were born with an eternal desire to fulfill our calling and purpose. We all have a deep need to know that our existence on earth matters. So every decision is pulled toward our destiny. This is a "God-centered" urge.

> *We conform to the expectations of people in order to be accepted by them. We barter away our destiny for belonging.*

On the other hand, there's a force pulling us away from our destiny—it's a "people-centered" urge. We all need to be loved. We crave acceptance within our family and belonging within our community. So we adapt. We conform to the expectations of people in order to be accepted by them. We barter away our destiny for belonging. Like Esau, we trade our inheritance for a bowl of soup.

All people experience these conflicting urges. But women experience them in a unique way. Females are created in the image of God, but spend a lifetime being told that they are subordinate to males in some sense. Women are created by Father God for an eternal destiny that is defined *only* by His call and her purpose, but they are shackled by the cultural norms and societal expectations of what a woman ought to be.

To get along, she goes along.

She is called to greatness, but consigned to subjection. Created to manifest God's image, but reduced to posture a propriety that the world demands. From girlhood on, she grows up with innate confusion and uncertainty. It creates a deep, existential conflict within the female heart, a cognitive dissonance that often degenerates into manipulation and resentment.

I know because I lived it. I grew up in the 1970s and 1980s, which was a time of profound change for women within American and Western culture. It was a confusing time. There were mixed expectations for me because I was a woman. Spoken and unspoken expectations. Some overt, jarring, and others subtle but insistent. The signals were convoluted, conflicting and often confusing.

But I also watched as the twentieth century world celebrated the collapse of gender barriers. I recall being frequently asked, "What do you want to be when you grow up?" As if I had real options. As if the world was my oyster, my stage, my yo-yo on a string. There was a clear expectation that I would be much more than a unpaid housekeeper, cook, cleaner and caregiver. I could be anything I wanted to be.

Yet—not so fast!—the domestic tasks of womanhood were still assumed as a given for most girls. "You want to be the first woman President? That's wonderful, pretty girl! Go for it. But while you're at it, go get me another glass of sweet tea, pretty please. And bring me one of those wonderful chocolate chip cookies you made in your Home Economics class. Good girl."

Mixed signals.

There was also an underlying current that being *feminine* meant you should never outshine your man. Stand by him, but never outshine him. Never upstage him. You're an accent, arm candy, a prop meant to make him look good at parties.

Girls should never be *too much*. Never *too* loud, *too* talented or *too* smart. And you certainly shouldn't make *too* much money. If a woman was more successful financially than her husband, it would diminish his prestige. People might scoff at him because his woman was supposed to be his subordinate.

Do you see the mixed signals? Signals that I could be anything I wanted—as long as I still managed the household well and didn't lose my "femininity" in the process. Powerful women, women who pushed past the cultural limitations and outshined the men in their orbit, were often characterized as "too manly," which is the nice way of saying it.

Powerful women were unattractive to the men, I was told. In those days, being "feminine" primarily meant that you needed to look good physically. Be thin, wear the appropriate amount of makeup, make sure your hair is done and wear flattering clothes that highlight your feminine physique without being provocative. Catch his eye, but don't make him feel insecure.

In the 1980s, most of the world around me was encouraging girls to go to college, get a degree and climb the corporate ladder. Shatter the glass ceiling. Be all you can be! But make sure while you do that you also keep the house clean and tend to the kids. Work eighty hours at the office and then come home and play June Cleaver. Apron on, supper done, dazzling smile for the man of the house. A truly successful woman manages it all.

Mixed signals.

A feminine woman maintains a soft, submissive demeanor even while climbing the ladder of success in her stylish heels.

This super woman was free to be successful, but not too successful.

She must know how to succeed in a dog-eat-dog workplace while maintaining a polished, cheerful attitude. An *accommodating* attitude. Be bold and competent, but never too aggressive. Get the contract, close the sale, crunch those numbers, plan the office Christmas party, collect those canned goods for the deserving poor. You go, girl! Change the world. But do it all with panache and *feminine* grace.

This super woman was free to be successful—if she could somehow pull it off under such impossible expectations—but not *too* successful. She had to tap the brakes just before racing past the man in her life. Rein it in. Don't embarrass him. Decline that promotion. Refuse that new job offer. Whatever you do, don't shame him.

Living with these conflicting expectations is a bit like living life in a minefield—always dodging between conflicting goals that could blow up at any moment and make life messy.

Do you see the quandary? Created by God to manifest His image, to display His glory; yet constrained by culture to maintain subordination and acquiescence. This is what gives rise to mixed feelings in women. This entire conundrum, this tension, this ambivalence, this equivocation—call it whatever nice word you want— arises from being pulled between two opposing forces: *creation* and *culture*.

Where Did We Get This Idea?

But hold on just one moment. How did we get here? Who gave us the idea that men are superior to women? Don't brush past this question. The male supremacy model of human society is so pervasive that it may at times seem like it's just how things were meant to be. But the longing for equality embedded deep within the female heart belies another, greater reality: male supremacy and female subjugation is not how God made the world. The mixed feelings within women betray an echo of a previous life, of a time when the world was undivided, when men and women were united as the image of God.

So here's the question again: how did we get here? When, where, how did we get the idea that men had to be superior to women? Where did society get the idea that a man was less of a man if the woman in his life outshined him in some area—especially in intellect or income? Where did we get the idea that successful women must downplay their accomplishments, simper demurely and play dumb just to get along?

You want to know where we got it? I'll tell you.

That idea was born from a lie, craftily devised by the father of lies himself. Satan invaded the Garden of Eden as a serpent who enticed the first humans to sin. Afterwards, when God confronted the humans and the snake who misled them, the awful reality of the curse sank down upon them. The serpent heard God say,

> *Because you have done this, cursed are you more than all cattle, and more than every beast of the field; on your belly you will go, and dust you will eat all the days of your life; and I will put enmity between you and the woman, and between your seed and her seed; He shall bruise you on the head, and you shall bruise him on the heel." (Genesis 3:14–15)*

And while the serpent was still writhing under the force of the curse—"the seed of the woman will crush your head!"—he heard God address the woman,

> *"I will greatly multiply your pain in childbirth, in pain you will bring forth children; yet your desire will be for your husband, and he will rule over you." (Genesis 3:16)*

The serpent froze. (He was cold-blooded anyway.) His eyes narrowed as he contemplated the Creator's broken-hearted words to the woman: "Your desire will be for your husband, and he will rule over you."

That's it, the serpent thought. His head swung slowly around to view the woman more directly. Once again, his eyes narrowed as his hatred for the woman rose like bile in his throat. The enmity God promised started coiling as a twisted plot within his serpentine mind.

"I will defeat the woman and prevent her seed from crushing my head by exploiting the rivalry between men and women and make them think that this is what the world should be like. In fact," the serpent whispered, sniggering to himself, "I will make humans think that the curse upon them was the Creator's intent. I will *religionize* (the serpent had a devilishly shrewd vocabulary) the curse. I will twist the curse of rivalry between male and female into 'the way the world ought to be' through religion. Yes-s-s-s-s!" he said as he slithered slowly away.

Admittedly, I may be taking a few liberties with the narrative, but I'm not far off.

The serpent left the Garden at war with the woman. He was "at enmity" with her. The serpent was desperate to scatter the woman's power, for her seed was destined to crush his head. So, how to stop her? He knew that he had to "divide and conquer," but how? By exploiting the rivalry between men and women provoked by the curse. By conning humans into believing that men were created to "rule over" women and that women were created to serve men. Satan "normalized" the rivalry—

and it was *never* meant to be normal. This fallacy originated in the Fall, and it has been perpetuated by nearly every culture and society since. It is a strategic perversion of the truth by mankind's greatest enemy.

And the most diabolical part of the plot was that satan successfully embedded this rivalry in religion. In fact, for millennia, satan's primary vehicle for carrying this sneaky little lie has been religion. He craftily embedded it into our forms of worship so he could keep us divided under the guise of righteousness. How better to institutionalize male supremacy than to say God wanted it that way? There's no lie more powerful than the one wrapped in a semblance of truth. Just like he did on that fateful day in the Garden, that old serpent still takes something true and twists it ever so slightly so we believe the lie. And what better way to twist the truth than to give it a religious twist?

Divided We Fall

The enemy's purpose and intent from the beginning of time is to get men and women to *divide*. And that's still true today. Of course, men and women are different. You've probably noticed. But those differences were meant to connect us, not divide us. That was the Creator's original design. God made us so that we would fit together like puzzle pieces. However, the enemy knows that our power to defeat him comes from our unity. So he works to divide us in every way possible.

It's quite simple, actually.

And so true that it's been immortalized as a truism:

"United, we stand; divided, we fall."

Now, some may object that the stark reality I'm describing has been long overcome by the advances made in gender relations over the last generation. And that's true to some extent, thankfully. I always want to honor the gains made by God-fearing suffragists and feminists, both men and women. The idea of male supremacy as the basis for human relationships has largely diminished in our secular society over the past few decades. That is surely evidence of a new Kingdom gaining sway in the world.

Women's lives have changed dramatically over the past 150 years, for sure. Women went from being treated like chattel— literally, like pieces of property owned by their fathers or husbands—to being valued as human beings. For

And the truly sad part is that inequality between men and women is most often found today in the place where that new Kingdom order should be most evident: the Church.

most of human history, women had no right to own property; no right to earn or keep wages; no right to enter into legal contracts; often not even the right to divorce if being abused. Women often had no more power than a slave had with his or her master. The woman was a mere accessory, simply a condiment for the main dish—desirable but dispensable. If the man was a sizzling New York Strip, then the woman was just Heinz 57.

Incredible.

So, yes, things have improved considerably. Yet, as it always is in a fallen world, chauvinism is still present to some degree. And the truly sad part is that inequality between men and women is most often found today in the place where that new Kingdom order should be most evident: the Church.

In fact, male superiority is not just present in the Church, it is still actively taught in many churches as God's intended design for humanity. It is presented as "God's order" for the family, church and society. And—if I may be so bold!—that idea must be exposed *here and now* as another lie straight from the serpent's mouth. The religious world has taken a deranged reality spawned from a lie and canonized it as church polity and practice. The traditional church has consecrated satan's most devious stratagem as its ecclesiastical structure.

But to be fair—and I definitely seek to be that!— satan was able to sell this lying bill of goods due to a sincere misunderstanding of Scripture. The devil twisted the interpretation of a few scriptures to get well-intentioned people to succumb to his evil plan of thwarting the establishment of God's Kingdom on earth. What we meant for good, satan meant for evil.

In today's modern church society, women are considered more equal in their humanity, but not in their role. If before we were merely a condiment, we have now at least become a side-dish. Now, if the man is New York Strip, then at least we've become mashed potatoes.

In some cases, even *garlic* mashed potatoes. With parsley garnish.

Fancy.

And what's wrong with that? I mean, after all, we have come such a long way! Why can't we women just be happy that we finally made it on the menu?

Here's why. Divided humans were never God's plan. God never intended for the man to be the main course and the woman to simply accompany him. God designed the two, male and female, to be one unit in His image. And His image—what God is like—provides our first clue of what He wants humans to be like. God is three in one: Father, Son and Holy Spirit. And He created male and female (and child) to manifest that one, undivided image.

The husband and wife are supposed to be *one*, just like the Father, Son and Holy Spirit are *one*. You see, it actually takes both man and woman coming together into unity to make one, sizzling Kingdom-steak. He's New. She's York. Together they are New York Strip.

As long as we divide, as long as we believe women are secondary to men, we reduce both men and women far beneath what God created them to be. And, tragically, we play right into the devil's scheme—his scheme to divide and conquer.

Why does this matter? Because the Kingdom of God cannot be established in the earth as long as it remains divided. And the Kingdom of God cannot be united until the Church is united. The Church cannot be united until men and women are united. I am not exaggerating when

I say that the full liberation and empowerment of women is essential to the coming of the Kingdom of God in the world. It's that important.

Think about the Church. It is still quite divided. And we all pray for the unity of the Body of Christ. But before unity can take place within the Church, between the various sects and denominations that express our unique worship traditions, unity must first happen at its nucleus, at its core.

The nucleus of the Church is its individuals and families. And, while we are taught to give lip service to Christian unity, in practice we are taught that men and women are divided. Whether this was taught in actual lesson plans in Sunday School or merely demonstrated in

> *And, while we are taught to give lip service to Christian unity, in practice we are taught that men and women are divided.*

everyday life, most Christians have been conditioned to believe that men have a higher role than women by God's design.

Again, we have made huge progress over the past century. Barely more than a hundred years ago in America women did not even have the right to vote. No say in how they were governed. The men simply made their choices for them. And that was normal. Seems unbelievable now, doesn't it? But that progress happened because of all the brave men and women who fought so hard against incredible prejudice and ignorance to achieve the liberty that most of us today simply take for granted.

Unexpected Consequences

Thank God for the changes we've seen. Sadly, however, there was an unexpected side effect to the liberties gained. As females gained the right to exist as people rather than possessions, a whole list of rights were *added* to the woman's experience of life. They were given the *added* right of voting, working and having a say in the world around them. But they were also expected to continue on with the responsibilities they previously carried. Women gained new rights, but there was no reciprocal shift of responsibilities where the men took on their part of what women had been carrying for generations. The men gave the women *added* rights, but then expected them to also keep right on as before.

There's those mixed signals again.

Taking on more responsibilities as they gained more rights would not have been a problem if all women were Wonder Woman. Or Supergirl. Or any female you can think of with superhuman abilities. But for those lowly women who are mere mortals—who knows, this may be you!—they found themselves feeling like they could never be enough. Being Supergirl without superpowers is exhausting.

And the liberated but now exhausted women eventually became hopeless and depressed. They became increasingly embittered and almost always ended up belittling and resenting their men. It got ugly.

What do you think happened to the men in those families? They were getting mixed signals too. On the one hand, they were happy to become "enlightened males" and let the girls gain more power. "Sure, go ahead and vote. Get a job. After all, the second income is nice. Take back your power. Just don't ask me to take over washing the dishes. I'm tired from working all day, and I just want to watch TV. Football is on."

The newly liberated women just wanted to get along, for the most part. So they accepted this new, "mixed signal" reality. And they tried hard at being Wonder Woman. But with an attitude. And that attitude hardened into outright resentment. The resentment grew and relationships soured.

The men reacted to the new reality. They were put off balance by the new regime. Many men were simply bewildered by the new rules introduced mid-game. Think about it now from the man's perspective. How would you feel if your partner were unappreciative or even resentful of you? How would you feel if your partner acted like they could take care of everything and didn't really need you? Feeling like you are dispensable and taken for granted deteriorates quickly into an empty state of existence.

Maybe at first you would simply disconnect emotionally to keep your sanity. Then, eventually, since you were nonessential and miserable, you would simply leave. And that's what many men did. They were thrown off balance, unsure of their role in this new, equal world. So they simply retreated. Gave up and walked away.

These men also didn't know what to do with the mixed signals.

Sadly, the ultimate casualties of all this was the children. Dad walked away, and the kids were left confused and broken. As they grew up in broken and fatherless homes, their father's absence, whether physical and/or emotional, created a void that no one else could fill. Then the kids got—you guessed it!—mixed signals.

Are you depressed yet? I truly hope not! But we must take a direct look at what the mixed signals did to our culture in order to understand how to get back to what God originally designed.

The Root of the Problem

Despite achieving greater levels of liberty for women in the land of the free, American families were not strengthened. In fact, we watched in horror as family units started completely breaking down. What should have made us stronger didn't. But why not? If half the population gained liberty and power, shouldn't the whole nation have risen in liberty and power? There seems to have been a root problem that wasn't solved by allowing women in the workforce or giving them the right to vote.

What was this "root problem"? I think it was the underlying assumption of male supremacy. Women obtained more power, but the deep-seated idea, pervasive in human culture since the Fall, that men are superior to women and women must "Wonder-woman" their way into equality was never really addressed. Men permitted women more equality, but it was handed out as if female empowerment was a privilege graciously granted by superior men.

No one says it quite like that, but that's the underlying idea that leads a man to sit on the couch watching TV while his wife comes in from work—the same hours he just worked!—and makes supper, helps with homework, bathes the kids and gets everyone in bed. The imbalance wasn't corrected because the underlying idea of male superiority was never fully addressed.

And the main reason it was never fully rooted out, even in secular culture, is that

> *To put it bluntly, the world can never be free from chauvinism as long as the Church provides it a sanctuary.*

religion preserved the old order in the place where it mattered most—the Church. To put it bluntly, the world can never be free from chauvinism as long as the Church provides it a sanctuary.

The root problem grows from a root idea, a core belief, that women were created by God to be secondary to their men. Many Christians have read the creation accounts in Genesis, together with Paul's teaching on gender roles, and accepted the traditional view that God created men superior. And I certainly understand that. As my story, which I'll share in the next chapter, shows so clearly, I get it! As a Christian, I believe the Bible is the Word of God and that it is to be used as our plumb-line in all of life. We *must* take what the Bible says seriously. Quite seriously.

But, as my story will also show, I came to understand that our interpretation of these passages has been terribly, tragically wrong. And since most Christians have been taught that women are to take a secondary role to men based on the misinterpretation of a few scriptures, we will deal with those passages in detail throughout this series.

How and why we got these scriptures mixed up is vitally important, so we cannot skim over the surface of these passages. We cannot skip the text or the context. We must drill down a bit. We must take the time to work through the difficult sections.

You see, the root problem—the gender issue—is not the main problem. It is a symptom of a greater problem. Male supremacy is not a problem just because it oppresses women—that's certainly bad enough—but because *it unleashes the wrong kingdom into the world.*[1]

The enemy has been at work establishing his kingdom, right alongside Christians as we work to establish God's Kingdom on earth. Just like the parable of wheat and the tares that Jesus talked about. (Matthew 13:24-30) Both kingdoms exist and grow side by side right under our nose. The fox is in the henhouse!

---

[1] "Wrong kingdom" has become shorthand for me to identify ideas that come from the kingdom of darkness. You'll see me use it often throughout this series.

It is important to understand that male supremacy at any level builds the wrong kingdom. As does female supremacy, by the way. It is time to recover the image of God revealed in male and female and allow the unity of man and woman to release the unity of heaven from the family to the Church to the Kingdom and to the world. It is time to unleash women and thereby unleash the Kingdom.

CHAPTER 2

IT ALL STARTS WITH A STORY

Before anyone yells, "Heresy!" in a crowded church building or starts throwing stones with deadly accuracy—and just before we dive into the nuts and bolts of the relevant scriptures—I would like to share a little of my own personal story.

I want you to know just a bit about me and my mandate. It's important for you to understand what compels me to write about such a controversial topic. I feel strongly that I have been given a divine assignment.

The Struggle Is Real

To be clear, I am not exaggerating the controversy surrounding this topic. If you attend a traditional evangelical or fundamentalist type church, you are well aware that a woman's secondary role in family and church is vehemently defended as God's will. Any opinion to the contrary is incredibly controversial. In fact, any attempt to question the validity of the gender hierarchy is met with fierce resistance.

In many circles, if you bring up evidence supporting a different point of view, it is automatically assumed you are in error. Without doubt, you *must* be taking scriptures out of context. Many traditionalists won't even examine the evidence to see if there is any validity to it. The secondary role of women is simply settled orthodoxy. Don't challenge it.

To many honest, sincere believers, gender equality in all respects must be opposed as heresy because "the Bible tells me so." They quote a handful of scriptures to support their view. They truly believe God intended women to be second and silent. And they believe that respecting this hierarchy honors God.

And yet there's a great deal of wobble in how traditionalist churches view the subjection of women. The inconsistency is striking. In the strictest, most conservative churches, the command for women to be "silent" is absolute. Nary a word from the estrogenous section. But in most evangelical and fundamentalist churches, the restriction for total silence has been qualified somewhat. Women are permitted to sing in the choir or teach children in Sunday School. Yet these more permissive traditionalist churches still use the scriptures commanding female "silence" in church to enforce compliance to a subjectionist (to create a word out of thin air!) order. Women are still assumed to be secondary to men, and the "keep silent" verses are used to justify that position. The inherent inconsistency of

> *The inherent inconsistency of using supposed biblical commands to be "silent" as support for being somewhat silent is generally ignored. Silence is not somewhat.*

using supposed biblical commands to be "silent" as support for being *somewhat* silent is generally ignored. Silence is not somewhat.

We will work through those verses in a bit.

Regardless of where your church comes down on all this, I am not being overly dramatic when I say that this topic is controversial. In much of the Christian world today, "the women issue" is as controversial as "the slavery issue" was in the nineteenth century. In fact, the successful abolition of slavery in Great Britain and the United States is largely what drove the suffragist movement from the Civil War era into the early years of the twentieth century. Equality for enslaved people led inexorably to the idea of equality for the other "enslaved people"—women.

How I would have loved for God to give me an easygoing assignment so I could make the whole world smile. But He didn't, so I can't. I can't for the same reason William Wilberforce couldn't. He couldn't just go along with the status quo on slavery in his day. He fought for the abolition of slavery in the British Parliament for decades. He had a divine assignment. The Kingdom of God was coming in the world, and Wilberforce was God's instrument for change.

Of course, I would never put myself in the same league as Wilberforce. Not for a second. Truthfully, I don't carry a fraction of the eloquence or zeal he carried. But I do understand his motives. Wilberforce believed the Lord called him.

And, if I may say so without seeming presumptuous, so do I. I believe I have been given a divine assignment to challenge the status quo and unleash the Kingdom fully by unleashing Kingdom women.

Those who know me well know that I am a reasonable person. And I yearn for peace and unity within the Body of Christ more than anything. I have prayed for unity since I was a brand new Christian. It has been a deep longing for me.

So then, why would such a reasonable person who wants unity more than anything take on the establishment and invite controversy? He or she wouldn't unless he or she was compelled to do so. That's where I am. After years and years of dealing with this subject—with most of that time spent trying to avoid it —the Lord always brings me right back here.

So here we are.

And this brings me back to my story. As I said above, I want to share some of my background so you can see why I believe I have a divine assignment.

Allow me then to introduce myself.

My Story

I was born in 1964 on the East Coast, in Maryland. In the late 1960s and through the 1970s, the formative years of my childhood and adolescence, the Women's Liberation Movement emerged as a powerful and influential cultural force. It had a profound impact on society's view and treatment of women.

Yet in the midst of significant change, with bursts of outright chaos, there was never to my recollection specific dialogue at home about women's liberation. My parents divorced when I was in elementary school. After that, we no longer lived in a traditional-style family with mom at home and dad at work.

I just remember feeling as a female that I should be able to handle anything and everything. There were two songs that I heard over and over, and they played repeatedly in my mind. The first was a catchy jingle for the *Enjoli* cologne commercial. It went like this:

I can bring home the bacon,
Fry it up in a pan,
And never let you forget you're a man,
'Cause I am a woman!

The other song playing repeatedly in my head was Helen Reddy's number one hit, "*I Am Woman.*" The powerful lyrics repeated this feisty phrase:

I am woman, hear me roar,
If I have to, I can do anything,
I am strong,
I am invincible,
I am woman.

I bet I played that Helen Reddy song at least a thousand times. In my mind, not only could I do *anything*, but I was supposed to do *everything*. I was supposed to take care of the home, and I was supposed to achieve success in the outside world. There's those pesky mixed feelings again.

You know how you ask a kid, "What do you want to be when you grow up?" Whenever someone asked me that question, I always answered it with one definitive answer: "A lawyer." That's all I ever remember wanting to be.

Then one day, as I was getting ready to go to college, a huge seed of doubt was planted in my heart about being ambitious or successful professionally. It was 1983, and my father made a statement that shocked me. He said, "The only reason for you to go to college is to find your husband." It surprised me because I had no clue he felt that way about me. He had never talked with me on a deep or personal level, so I didn't realize that he had *no* aspirations for me professionally. The truth was, I had always wanted to be an attorney like him.

I was shaken by his words. But I had no other plan for my life. So I went on to school, and four years later I graduated. I didn't meet my husband at college, but I did quit applying to law schools shortly thereafter when I met the man I was going to marry. I guess Dad's words were more accurate than I wanted to believe.

Another time I glimpsed my father's view of women when a female friend of his decided to run for Governor. She was well suited for the job. Many years earlier, when I was just a toddler, she had helped my father run for a seat in the U.S. Congress. He didn't win, but they stayed in touch over the years.

At the news of her gubernatorial candidacy, I could imagine her going even further. I said excitedly, "How awesome would it be if she were to become President one day?" Dad turned quickly and emphatically stated that he would *never* vote for a woman to be President, not even his good friend. Stunned, I asked, "Why not?" Dad declared firmly and unequivocally that a woman should *never* be President *because the Bible said so!*

My dad was a smart, well-read man, but he was not spiritual. He went to church for social and professional reasons, but he was a Christian in name only. He chose his church because, in his words, "That's where the good people go." Meaning the more affluent.

Jesus was not Dad's Lord or Savior. Dad claimed that he was agnostic. He didn't think that anyone could really *know* God, not in any personal way. He supposed that the way to Heaven (if there really was one) was simply to be a good person. He did not believe the Bible. In fact, he rejected the biblical narrative that salvation comes through Jesus' sacrifice and atonement. He doubted that Jesus was born of a virgin and that He was raised from the dead. In fact, my dad would often poke fun at the religious people who believed such things.

Since he did not speak openly with me about his opinion of women or their role in the world, I was honestly surprised to learn he didn't think a woman should ever hold that level of office. But what totally shocked and confused me was the fact that he used the *Bible* as the reason for his position. He had read the Bible, but he openly did not believe it. Since he didn't think the Bible was true, why would he use it to support a dismissive, even derogatory, position toward women?

In hindsight, I have come to understand that society at large uses the Bible when it is convenient to support their preferred point of view. When change-resistant people need a basis for preserving the status quo, there is no better status quo authority than the Bible— selectively interpreted, of course. When the Women's Liberation Movement started yanking down the long established structures of patriarchal society, the defenders of the old order waxed eloquent quoting Scripture.

Even for people who were not particularly religious, the Bible conveniently became the primary support for the philosophy that women were designed to be secondary to men and that their proper role was to stay at

> *Society at large uses the Bible when it is convenient to support their preferred point of view.*

home, bake cookies and raise the kids. The Bible does not actually teach this, which this series will prove beyond a shadow of a doubt. However, because this was mankind's mindset, they interpreted and translated the Bible that way. It became a self-fulfilling prophecy.

Now here was my dad doing the same thing!

Back then, I had no clue of how people selectively used the Bible to support preconceived ideas. I just knew something didn't feel right about my dad's position. It didn't ring true. It contradicted what the world taught me. How could I be "anything, strong and invincible" but with a glass ceiling?

However, I had not read the Bible, so I didn't know. Perhaps he was right. An internal conflict began to brew in my heart. It was rather silent and subtle, but it was there playing in the background.

A Radical Spiritual Transformation

Fast forward two decades. At age thirty-five, my reasoning totally shifted when I experienced a radical spiritual transformation. My outlook on life, my worldview, my paradigm, everything that shaped my way of viewing the world, was fundamentally restructured from the ground up. I truly became a believer.

When I was very young, my mom had raised me to believe in Jesus and the gifts of the Holy Spirit. As a child, I said the Sinner's Prayer and was baptized. I believed in Jesus. *I really did!* However, everything I believed could fit on a Hallmark card. It was simple, short and sweet. I accepted that Jesus was the Son of God. I trusted that He died for my sins. He was born on Christmas and raised on Easter. I genuinely believed, but that's about all I understood.

More importantly, I didn't know Jesus personally. I lived with my dad through junior high and high school. So I grew up maturing in the world outside the Church. In my heart I trusted that Jesus was real, but it was mostly the world that influenced my thinking.

By the age of thirty-five, I was married with two wonderful kids (Ben and Jaclyn), and, ironically, it was my kids that drew me back to a deeper hunger for God. I had put them in a Christian school because, even though we were not a church-going family, I wanted them to be taught the tenets of the faith. And I watched as my children developed a relationship with God that I didn't have.

I was getting hungry.

Both my kids were learning the Bible and came to know that Jesus truly loved them. I was drawn in by their affection and understanding of God. Something came alive inside me. It was like I suddenly tapped into my purpose for being on the planet. I began attending the church where they attended school. I went every time the doors were open. I devoured the Bible, reading it from cover to cover. I participated in every Bible study class I could find. I was eager to know Him and to learn everything I could. I loved it!

However, I soon ran into a problem. In my world outside the church, women could become anything they aspired to be. (At least idealistically.) Young girls were growing up to believe now that the sky was the limit. Maybe my dad was wrong—maybe a woman could be President one day. After all, President Ronald Reagan had appointed Sandra Day O'Connor as the first female Supreme Court Justice. To my knowledge, that seemed to be going along well. At least the world hadn't come to an end because a woman got above herself.

My generation was the first to fully attempt living out the breathtaking promise of the Declaration of Independence, the inalienable right to life, liberty and the pursuit of happiness, for all people. Black people and white people. Rich people and poor people. And now, male people and female people.

No longer were these inalienable rights merely given to aristocratic, white males. We believed everybody had the opportunity to be a success, to make their dreams come true, to be a world changer—*everybody!* You might have to overcome extreme challenges and hardships, but the field of life was now open to everyone serious about the game. And that field was now more level than it had ever been.

However, I began experiencing a new dilemma. A whole new set of *mixed signals*. Without warning, I began to feel a strong call to ministry. Which was a bit awkward—in my church, ministry was not open to women. No matter that I had a good education, strong job history in the workplace and even managerial experience. Regardless how qualified I was in the outside world, in the church I was disqualified *simply for being a woman*. That was awkward indeed.

Maybe, since you're just getting to know me, I should back up my claims of being qualified. Would that help? Then indulge me as I wave my resume around just a bit.

My Resume

Prior to having kids, I worked through high school and college. My first job was as a school janitor. I started working there when I was only fifteen. It wasn't long before I switched to an office job working for a female entrepreneur who built a software development company. I did everything in the office from accounting and payroll to testing and documentation. In college, I added a second job working with a small retail shop in a large mall and was soon promoted to assistant manager. My manager at the store was also a woman.

Then I went to college and earned my bachelor's. After graduation, I took the LSAT's and began applying to law schools. That's when I met my first husband. His family owned a small antique business, and he wanted me to help them. Becoming a lawyer would have been too all-consuming, so I shelved those aspirations.

Instead, I accepted a professional position at a large military contracting corporation. I worked hard, and within a short period of time was promoted to supervising a support team. My immediate boss was a female, and her boss was also a female. Having all those female bosses wasn't planned. I had no idea I would be working for women when I took the job. It never came up in the interviews with Human Resources.

Just being in the workplace, I experienced women in positions of power and authority. It became familiar to me, so naturally I intended to become one of them. It was perfectly acceptable. Why wouldn't you want to be as successful as you could be? For me, it was not just about making money. I wanted to have significance and value. I wanted to make a difference and bring positive change to the world around me. In my professional experience, there was nothing negative or detrimental about a woman serving in leadership.

In previous generations, it would have been nearly impossible for a woman to attain the levels of leadership I experienced. I know now by looking at workplace statistics from those years that I was naïve, sheltered and living in my own little bubble surrounded by women leaders. But from what I personally witnessed and experienced in the workplace, advancement was based on *merit.* And merit was measured by my productivity, by my creativity, by leadership

> *Staying home was deemed less valuable than climbing the corporate ladder. How could you make a difference in the world if you stayed at home?*

and loyalty—not on race, or gender or social status. The playing field was level, as I saw it.

Based on my experience up to this point, I figured if I worked hard enough, I could do anything. After all, like the anthem roared,

I am strong,
I am invincible,
I am woman!

Following the birth of my first child, Benjamin, my heart yearned to stay home. As I held my infant son, looking into his sweet face, I could not imagine anyone else taking care of him all day. But in the world's view, in the corporate attitude of my co-workers, staying home was deemed less valuable than climbing the corporate ladder. How could you make a difference in the world if you stayed at home? The professional world did not esteem the role of a wife and mother.

This clash of competing value systems around me caused a conflict within me. To gain significance in the world, I had to prove my success as a professional. I had to demonstrate again and again that I was a competent leader. Leadership as a category of self-development was becoming the latest craze, and to stay home meant that I was abdicating my responsibility as a leader. Dropping the ball, letting the team down.

And yet. My mother's heart ached to be at home with Ben. So guess what I did? That's exactly what I did. I quit my job. I followed my heart.

Two and half years later, I was doubly blessed as my daughter, Jaclyn, burst into our family so full of life and beauty. I loved my children deeply, and I was incredibly grateful that I had the financial ability to choose to stay home and be their main caregiver.

I still helped with the family business and found other work I could do from home to make some money, but it never felt the same. Although I enjoyed the rewards of being a mother, it felt when I gave up my career that I had lost my identity and my ability to make a difference in the world. And it felt that way until I had my radical encounter with Christ and plugged into that

Bible-believing church, the same one I mentioned before that brought such blessing into the lives of my children.

Here's what changed. In this church, I soon discovered to my delight, stay-at-home moms were highly esteemed. This small group of believers taught openly and often about the value of family to the world. I found a new sense of significance and value for my daily service in life. I could actually make a difference in the world by pouring myself into my home.

Family matters! It mattered significantly at my new church. Thanks to my newfound faith community, I was now able to put into words why my heart yearned so much to stay home. As a result of my choice to put family first, I experienced a different level of freedom and value as a stay-at-home mom that I could not find in the world outside the church.

By the way, I should pause and say this now, lest you misunderstand me: stay-at-home moms—stay-at-home dads too!—what you do is so important. Your service is valuable. Not just to your family, but to society at large and to God's Kingdom. You are shaping lives and building the next generation.

And for those who want to stay home but cannot, I offer zero condemnation. Single income families have it tough, especially in single parent homes. God will see you through this important season of your life. Just ask Him. He will help you protect and nurture your children. Never abdicate your role as primary caregiver for your children, even if someone else is watching them while you work. You are the one called and gifted to raise your own children and to be the godly role model they need. You are their number one influence.

How, you may ask, can I be their number one influence when I have to drop them off each day for others to watch while I work? That's a tough question, and I would never minimize your concern. But, truthfully, I think the best way to be the number one influence in their lives is by staying connected heart to heart. Use the time you *do* have together to connect on a heart level. You cannot *tell* them how to love and how to live—you must *show* them day in and day out. Your connection with their heart will survive long past all the dinners, chores, schooling, sports and friends. Being a parent, whether you get to do it full-time or not, is a vital, life-changing role.

Anyway, it was so refreshing to be in a community where I was valued for a choice that so many disdained. But as always, there was a flip side. It did not take me long to discover that being a wife and mom was *all* this church esteemed for women. It did not matter if a female was gifted or anointed, there were restrictions placed on her solely because of her gender. And, since I was feeling a burgeoning call within my spirit, an altogether different internal conflict began to brew.

A Burgeoning Call

God was now putting dreams and desires in my heart for ministry that made no sense in this environment. Being female, I could not be in leadership. I could not manage. I could not even teach, unless the setting was restricted to other women or children. There was a clear division between the adult men and everyone else.

A thick glass ceiling was hanging heavy over the church I loved, a ceiling that had not been present in my workplace. Of course, in many American work environments the glass ceiling was still there—just covert, cleverly disguised. But here at my church, it was overt, out in the open and justified as God's plan for humanity. Honestly, it felt strange to gain freedom in some areas just to lose it in others.

Let me be clear. That first church was wonderful in so many ways. Because it was decidedly a fundamentalist church, the leaders were superb at teaching the Bible. Many of the Sunday School classes were better

> **If the Word says something is true, then I believe it. And that settles it.**

than the classes I later took in seminary. They were deep and incredibly thorough. Most of all, they taught me to fully appreciate the Bible as the Word of God. They trained me to measure everything against the Word. I still do. The Bible is my plumb line.

That is one thing I want you to be sure of as we begin this journey together. *Unleashing the Kingdom* may be revolutionary, but it is still biblically sound. There is nothing in this book that goes against the Word of God. If the Word says something is true, then I believe it. And that settles it.

CHAPTER 3

WHY SEND MARY?

L ike so many other churches, the one I attended at the time believed the Bible taught that women must be under a male covering. Women could not be in positions of authority, nor could they teach adult men. That was their standard.

At first, I believed what they said was true. As I began to study the Word of God, I initially saw exactly what they were saying. There are several scriptures which seem at first glance to strictly prohibit women from leadership. For example, Paul says in his first letter to the Corinthian church,

> *Women shall keep silent in the church; for they are not permitted to speak. (1 Corinthians 14:34)*

And again, while writing to Timothy, the Apostle Paul says,

> *I permit not a woman to teach or have authority over a man. (1 Timothy 2:12)*

That is pretty clear, isn't it?

I would question scriptures like this regarding the women issue only so I could fully grasp and understand the church's position. It was not that I did not believe them; I just wanted to understand why and how to apply them. For example, Paul had several women on his ministry teams—how could he do that?

As I wrestled with understanding the reasoning and applications behind the prohibitions, I started asking leaders and members in my church about it. It surprised me when I was often met with strong, negative reactions. To them, the fact that women were to be secondary to men was clearly established as biblical fact; it was true and not to be debated. Judging by the intensity of their reactions, you would have thought I was questioning the validity and power of the cross.

However, I was willing to accept their interpretation, and even argue their case to others, if I could fully comprehend it. My questioning was not meant to be rebellious, honest to God, even though it got me in a few heated discussions. I was just trying to make the biblical position my own. Obviously, our church leaders were more experienced, and I trusted them. I was one hundred percent willing to embrace and defend the proposition that women are required by God to be silent in church and must never be permitted to occupy key roles of authority. I was willing to say so just because the Bible said so. But in my heart, I just wanted to understand the "so" the Bible actually said.

The mixed signals had me mixed up.

I was confused by so many inconsistencies. Like this: we had a home group at the time, and I was always playing this odd game of pretending that the principal male was leading when I knew he wasn't—I was. He never had the message or lesson ready. Neither did he seem to have any real desire to lead the group or the discussion. He would inevitably defer to me, and I would lead the group by stealth, as unobtrusively as I possibly could. That, together with the inconsistencies I saw in the Bible, were starting to really bother me.

At this point in time, if you had asked me to take a stand on the women's issue, I would have boldly declared what I thought the Bible said: "Women are to take a back seat. They are not to have key roles of authority because the Bible says so." I figured my dad must have been right after all.

That all changed in one moment.

A Simple Question

One day, the Lord asked me one simple question, and it turned me around on a dime. I wish now I had recorded the exact date, but it was sometime in the year 2000, that much I remember. It was still early in my Christian walk.

Regardless, I'll never forget that moment. I had just dropped the kids off at school, pulled back in the garage and got out of the car. I was headed toward the kitchen door when I heard the Lord ask me a question. It stopped me dead in my tracks. I remember exactly the spot where I was standing when the Lord spoke to me. It was not an audible, external voice, but it was very clear. It was the Lord speaking, and I knew it. I froze and my whole being came to attention.

"Susan," he gently asked, "why would I send Mary, knowing they would not believe her?"

The Father's words came with an instant, deep "knowing." I just knew immediately without explanation that He meant Mary Magdalene. And I knew the exact event to which He was referring: the announcement of His resurrection from the dead.

Wow.

I had to pause and process for a moment. If it was not right for women to teach or deliver Kingdom revelation to men, then why would Jesus have sent Mary Magdalene to the male disciples with the greatest, most important revelation ever spoken: "He is risen!" Why would He do that? The single most important announcement ever uttered, the greatest message ever preached entrusted to a woman—utterly breathtaking!

> *Why would He send Mary to give that message to a group of grown men knowing that they would not believe her?*

Jesus specifically chose a woman first to deliver the first and greatest sermon of all time.

Why? Why would He send Mary to give that message to a group of grown men knowing that they would not believe her? Truthfully, I had never given that question a single thought, but Jesus had. He knew full well the disciples would not believe her, and yet He sent her anyway. At the core, His question to me was, "Why would I do that, Susan?"

As you know, God's voice comes with His presence. When He speaks, "Peace!" you don't just hear the word "peace," you experience peace. So when He spoke, I received a revelation, an understanding, and I felt a deep sense of immediate certainty. Somehow, I just knew He wanted me to see that:

1) It was okay for a woman to deliver this amazing message.

2) That He had intentionally chosen her to do so.

3) That what I currently believed about "the women's issue" was wrong.

The Lord's one piercing question began to challenge and change my thinking. My assumptions started unraveling. Please understand it was not *the question itself,* "Why would I send Mary?" as much as it was *the fact that He was asking.* He was prompting me to question my beliefs. He was setting me up, inviting me to go on a mission, a wild adventure, a glorious journey with Him. He does that, you know—He just sets us up in a beautiful way.

Picture this. I'm standing stock-still in the garage. My mind is whirling, my heart is racing. I am profoundly, infinitely aware that I have just had a heaven-breaks-through moment. Like Jacob at Bethel. It is surreal, to say the least. But then my analytical, academic gifts kick in, and I start trying to regain my wits and plot my next move. I take a deep breath and murmur slowly,

"Okay, now I clearly know God's heart! I'm going to go in the house, open up my Bible, pull out some Greek lexicons, and find the proof that we have it all wrong."

If only it had been that simple.

Back to Scripture for a Closer Look

I thought, since I now know God's heart, reinterpreting His Word should be easy. I thought that this earth-shattering revelation would be like a pair of magic spectacles that would unveil the hidden secrets of Scripture that we'd all missed. Sort of like finding the key to the treasure map, the cipher for the code. After all, God just spoke to me!

I went in the house, opened my Bible and looked up all the relevant scriptures, cross references, definitions, you name it, hoping to find some evidence to prove what I now knew in my heart to be true. I now understood that God's heart did not match my theology. But the problem was I could not find the smoking gun—at least not at first. That day, as I was doing my research, I felt like I stumbled into quicksand. I was sinking with no way out.

It was awful.

Here was my problem. 1 Corinthians 14:34 plainly says,

> *"Women are to keep silent in church; for they're not permitted to speak."*

I read it again. It still said the same thing. No magic-spectacle-thing at all. I thought, "Okay, let's dig into the Greek. The answer must be hidden in the Greek!" But as I looked up the Greek words, I realized my effort to prove I'd heard God's heart was going downhill fast.

It was no better in the Greek than it was in English. If anything, it got worse. The word translated "silent" in this verse comes from the Greek root verb "*sigao.*" It means "to be or to become silent; to be hidden or concealed." What is astounding is that this word is used twice in the Greek at the beginning of the verse, even though it is only translated once in the English. A more accurate rendering would be, "Silence your women! Keep them silent in church!"

That was even more harsh than I had been taught.

Then the word rendered "speak" comes from the Greek word "*laleo,*" which simply means "to speak or to talk." So, three times in this one verse it clearly states that women are not to have any sound come out of their

> **Many modern-day proponents of male-only leadership in the Church would say that Paul really didn't mean what he said.**

mouth in church. The text is literally saying, "Silence your women! Keep them silent, for women are not permitted to have any sound coming out of their mouth in church, no sound at all!"

That seems pretty darn clear, doesn't it?

Many modern-day proponents of male-only leadership in the Church would say that Paul really didn't mean what he said. There's no way, they would say, that women could not talk or sing or speak at all. Rather, what the Apostle meant was that women should not voice their opinion or teach adult men. But that is not at all what the verse says. At all. The verse literally says women must be silent and not make any sound. It was not about dampening female opinions or influence. It was about totally silencing the female voice.

The following verse, verse thirty-five, says,

> *If they desire to learn anything, let them ask their own husbands at home; for it is improper for a woman to speak in church. (1 Corinthians 14:35)*

The plain statement of this text is that women are not even allowed to ask a question in church—forget making a statement or preaching a sermon. *Women were not even allowed to ask a question!*

From where I was sitting, things just went from bad to worse. It was super distressing. I would sit for hours, thinking, praying, processing all this with the Lord. I would ask questions like, "Okay, I know in my heart what You are saying to me, but what I'm seeing in your Word looks even more restrictive! Women are not even permitted to make any sound in church?! No sound at all—not even ask a question? Seriously?!"

It seemed bizarre. That was even more derogatory than I ever imagined. In fact, it was significantly more discriminatory than what even my church practiced.

I began to wonder, why do we allow women to sing in the choir? Singing is sound coming out of the mouth. Singing is not silent. Why were we letting women be on the worship team or teach young children?

The more I thought on that, the more it made no sense. Especially women being restricted to teaching young children. Think about it: why do we let women teach *young* children? Aren't children the most vulnerable among us, and if women cannot be trusted to teach, then why should we give them our most easily influenced? Indeed, in many churches the rationale for women being restricted from teaching men is based on Paul's statement in 1 Timothy 2:14, which appears to say women are uniquely susceptible to deception. Just like what happened when Eve ate the "apple."

So back to my question: if it is true that women are more easily deceived, then why would we allow them to teach the most vulnerable, the young and impressionable (who may not recognize error), but not teach the older and wiser (who should know better)? To go even further, why should we allow women to teach other women (who are more easily deceived) but not teach the men (who should more readily recognize error).

Not one shred of that made sense to me.

It took several years after that *eureka* moment in my garage for the Lord to fully lift the veil from my understanding and show me how I had gotten it so wrong. It was quite a journey.

Along the way, I began to see more and more how our application of these admonitions was selective and even blatantly contradictory. For example, my particular church did not require women to wear head coverings. Yet in 1 Corinthians 11:6 it clearly states, with the same apparent vigor as in Chapter 14, that women must cover their head while praying or prophesying. It further stated that the head covering was a symbol of submission to authority. Our church did not do that. We simply did not obey Paul's teaching.

It also struck me as I read back through the texts for the thousandth time that there was in inherent contradiction hidden in the command for women to cover their heads while praying or prophesying—they were to cover their heads *while praying or prophesying!* But how can women pray and prophesy while being silent? Makes no sense.

Again, I took all this to God. I was concerned that we were not obeying the clear teaching of Scripture regarding the head covering. I sincerely wanted to please the Lord. I prayed from the depths of my heart, "Lord, I will do whatever it is You want me to do, and I will honor You. I will cover my head if You want me to, but this just does not make any sense at all. Please help me to understand Your heart."

I was willing. I meant it. Head coverings were not totally foreign to me. There were numerous Amish and Mennonite communities around where I lived, and I had to admit that they were adhering to the letter of the law better than we were. But something just still seemed off to me. I was willing to wear the covering—and I would still! Honestly, I would cover my head for Jesus if I thought that is what He wanted me to do. I really would, and I bet you would too if you thought that was important to God.

But the larger question pulling my heart apart was our selective application of the Scriptures. It seemed disingenuous to me, though I believed that the hearts of our leaders were sincere. Over the next few months and years, I became completely embroiled in the struggle to figure out our selective application:

Why do we allow women to uncover their heads, but yet we do not allow them to teach adult men? Why pick one restrictive verse but not the other?

Some argued that the head coverings requirement was merely cultural, for that time period only. But if we can explain head coverings away with the cultural relevance argument, then why not do the same with the restrictions on women teaching? What evidence do we have within the texts that indicates which teachings we keep and which teachings we throw away?

All this bothered me profoundly. It seemed to me, the more I thought about it, that the Church simply wanted to preserve the restrictions on women teaching for their own reasons. Maybe the status quo was more important than we cared to admit.

A journey of a thousand miles begins with one small step. That small step for me was that gestalt moment in my garage. And thus began my long journey of a thousand miles, a thousand miles of unraveling deep mystery, a journey that still continues in some sense to this day.

There was a vast chasm between what I knew to be God's heart and what I saw in His Word. I knew in my gut that the chasm did not exist in reality, just in my understanding. So I went on a quest to find where I was wrong. I read books and articles. I studied the Word. I even called a number of different, well-known ministries to ask them about the basis for their varying positions regarding women in ministry.

I do not mind telling you that the journey of a thousand miles was the journey of a million frustrations. It took me six long years just to get from my initial starting point to a place where I could prove with confidence that what God said to me in my garage did *not* contradict what God said in His Word. It truly was okay for Him to send Mary on that first Sunday of a new Kingdom age. And it truly is okay today for Him to send women. I assure you it is!

In fact, the unity of men and women is a major key in the establishment of God's Kingdom on earth. The

> *In fact, the unity of men and women is a major key in the establishment of God's Kingdom on earth. The women's issue is really the women-and-men-together issue.*

women's issue is really the women-and-men-together issue. We're going to talk more about all that and prove it beyond a shadow of a doubt. I want you—especially if you are a God-called woman struggling with what the Bible says about your call—to be fully persuaded and confident that the Word of God supports your call. God didn't make a terrible mistake when He made you a woman and then called you to carry His Word. As we go along, we will walk together through all the evidence proving that the equality-in-unity of women and men is essential to the coming of Christ's Kingdom.

God did not create the female to play a merely secondary, assistant-type role. You are not some glorified Vanna White! No disrespect to Vanna, but you were not created to just look cute and smile while God works all around you through powerful men. No, He made *you* to be powerful.

You will see that there is absolutely *nothing* innate in women that caused the Fall. Women can be trusted with truth. Femininity is not a character flaw. Femininity is part of God's design for humanity. Likewise, masculinity is not something to be feared or controlled. Both are necessary for human leadership to reflect the full image of God in the home, in the world and in the Church. Both masculine and feminine attributes need to be fully present and honored.

So why did God send Mary? Everything God does has a purpose, and Jesus sent Mary for a reason. He was shattering the old mindset that women could not be trusted with revelation. In the culture of that day, Jesus should have sent a man to proclaim the greatest message ever delivered. Yet He did not, and He did not on purpose.

Many in Christendom today still believe God created the woman as a gift to the man, as his "helper." As we shall see in Book 3, this false idea so twists and perverts God's purposes that individual destinies are diminished and even destroyed. Worse yet, the manifestation of God's Kingdom is weakened and delayed on the earth.

Does that seem radical? I understand. It did to me as well when I first started hearing what Father God was saying. But sometimes it takes a radical word to break through the fossilized structures of human tradition. No matter how edgy this message may seem to you now, please do not be scared off by the radical call of this series. God has a powerful revelation embedded here. Don't miss it!

Just because you were always taught something, or just because everyone you know believes it, does not make that something true. Ever heard about people believing the earth was flat? Some still do, I have been told! But, thankfully, that's pretty rare. Today most of us have no doubt that the earth is round. And the ancient flat-earther's could have known it was true much earlier if they would have simply taken the Word of God at face value, for Isaiah 40:22 speaks of "He who sits above the *circle of the earth.*" God's Word never claimed a flat earth; it claimed a round one. The book of Isaiah had been around for more than two thousands years before Magellan ever set sail.

Why did they miss it? Tradition. So, since the "flat earth" issue for our generation is "the women's issue," we cannot cling to an idea just because it is a popular theory. Those who play it safe never leave the harbor. There's a better way: test the Word and prove God's faithfulness and truth for yourself.

Ready? Let's go deeper.

CHAPTER 4

CANCEROUS CHALDEE

At the beginning of 2006, I moved from Maryland to Texas. That's a long story all by itself. Another time. Anyway, later that same year, on a trip back East, I had a dream that changed my life.

She Has Chaldee!

I am not normally a big dreamer. I mean, of course, I have big dreams—huge dreams, in fact!—but I don't often have significant dreams at night. I am more of a studier. I am a left-brain, analytical type who enjoys looking up definitions and processing things logically. That is my norm. Dreams are unusual for me. If a dream grips me and stays with me hours or days after waking, then I know it is from God.

Back to this powerful, heart-stopping dream. It was very simple and very short. As I awoke out of a dead sleep, my heart was racing, and my whole body was quivering. I was literally panicked.

At the time of the dream, I had two dogs in real life, a pair of Dobermans. They were named Priscilla and Aquila after the famous wife and husband teaching team mentioned in four New Testament books.[1] Since my

---

[1] Priscilla (Prisca) and Aquila: See Acts 18:2, 18, 26; Romans 16:3; 1 Corinthians 16:19; 2 Timothy 4:19.

"Why send Mary?" encounter, I had developed an even greater desire to preach, teach and write. But I still was unclear as to exactly what my role could be because of my gender. In hindsight, I suppose naming my female dog "Priscilla" was a prophetic act of faith. We got her first. If Priscilla in the Bible could teach, then perhaps so could I. A couple of years later, Aquila joined our family.

In this dream, Priscilla (*aka* Prissy) was in some kind of large institutional building. Just inside the lobby was a counter. Behind it stood a woman wearing a white lab coat as if she was officially part of this institution. She was dressed like a doctor, and she held a clipboard with Prissy's medical chart on it. At the bottom of the clipboard was written "C-H-A-L-D-E-E" in huge, three or four-inch letters.

In the dream, I was extremely upset with this woman. I could clearly see that there was a huge problem spelled out on Prissy's chart, but the woman kept acting as if everything was fine. I stood there pointing across the counter at her clipboard, shouting, "No! No! No! It is *not* okay! Prissy is not okay! *She has CHALDEE!*" However, the white-coated woman just stood there looking at me with this oblivious mannequin-like, Stepford-wife-ish smile, as if to say, "Everything's okay. Everything's fine." However, things were not even close to *fine!* The woman was completely blind to the fact that there was a serious, even catastrophic, problem.

Don't patronize *me, lady!*

I remember waking up with my heart beating out of my chest. My whole body was shaking. I never had a dream affect me like that. Of course, I immediately asked the Lord, "What was *that?* What are You trying to tell me? And what in the world does *Chaldee* mean?"

The dream haunted me. I could not get the searing image of the woman's face and the clipboard with *CHALDEE* out of my head. Nor could I shake the overwhelming sense that something was terribly wrong.

Christian Woman Has Chaldee

Remember now, I was still wrestling with what the Bible taught regarding women in leadership and working to balance that with the "Why send Mary?" message I knew God had said to me in my garage. My research had uncovered stacks of pro-female verses and scriptural examples of women being used powerfully by God, but I still could not shake off the negative ones, the "clear prohibitions" of women leading. How could I violate something that was clearly written in the Bible, right there in black and white, even though I knew God was trying to tell me something different? Amidst the confusion, I was reluctant to move forward until I could biblically answer the question, "How free am I to preach God's message?"

But this dream was another big shift. Through it, God jolted me forward with an awakened sense of urgency. This message was not a gentle voice stopping me in my tracks like the time in my garage. This was a shocking, even fearful, experience. I was profoundly shaken.

Later, while visiting some friends, I shared the dream hoping to get an interpretation. One person quickly knew by the Spirit that Priscilla meant "Christian woman." That rang true in my heart. I could see that: in the dream "Priscilla" meant "Christian woman." Okay, got that.

So it seemed, as best as I could tell, that God was telling me that the problem was that "Christian woman has *Chaldee*." However, that did not help me understand the dream any better. "Who is the Christian woman? Is it me? Is it someone else? Is it all Christian women? And what in the world does *Chaldee* mean?"

My first reaction was to do my normal left-brain, pull out the concordances and do all the intellectual study stuff. Here is what I found: *Chaldee* was the language of the ancient Chaldeans who lived in Chaldea. Simple enough. But that rang a bell. I remembered reading in Genesis that Abraham came out of the city Ur, which was in Chaldea. So the idea of "Chaldee" went back before the time of Abraham, before there was a Hebrew nation. It seemed likely that there would be some sort of implicit connection between the land and the language of the Chaldeans and my dream, but it wasn't immediately obvious. And I still had no clear idea what "Christian woman has *Chaldee*" meant.

I also did not understand why I was so upset. Seriously, without even knowing fully what *Chaldee* meant, my heart was intensely troubled. I knew the message of the dream was significant, and I knew it was very important to God that I grasp what it meant. Yet, at that point, I simply could not get further clarification.

Complementarians & Egalitarians

Later, after returning to Texas, I "coincidentally" signed up for an online course called, *"God's Release of Women."* The course was offered by Christian Leadership University, led by Mark and Patti Virkler.[2] By the way, I strongly recommend Mark's books, *4 Keys to Hearing God's Voice* and *Dialogue With God.* I think every new believer's class should use them because so many Christians walk through life struggling to hear God. Too often, we neither recognize nor honor the voice of the One we serve.

Anyway, prior to taking the CLU course, I always felt uncomfortable when studying the women's issue. No matter which side I was currently looking at, it always seemed like something was wrong. Too often, the arguments were circular in nature, arguing 'round and 'round like a puppy chasing its tail. So many patronizing, "If you don't believe me, ask me!" kinds of arguments. Assumptions grew thick as weeds. Presuppositions slammed headlong into prejudicial postulations. *Ad hominem* attacks *ad nauseam*. It was messy, and I was getting frustrated.

Just to show you how silly and self-validating some of the arguments were, I remember reading one guy argue that God created two genders, male and female; therefore, equality between the sexes was inherently

---

[2] http://www.cluonline.com

impossible. Since there are two genders, he bravely surmised, one *must* be above the other. You have to wonder, as he scratched out his gender-math on a scholarly notepad, why he assumed that males were necessarily the "one" set above the other. Why not the other way around? I know a feminist or two that would *love* to challenge his chauvinist calculus.

But take a moment and be honest with me: does that sort of calculus sound like the Kingdom of Heaven? I mean, truly, is that even godly? Does that fit with your vision of the new creation? It certainly does not fit with mine.

> *Sadly, while researching, I often found that the spirits behind both sides of the debate were coming from the wrong kingdom.*

It all left me feeling confused and even somewhat discouraged. Sadly, while researching, I often found that the spirits behind *both* sides of the debate were coming from the wrong kingdom. After reading their arguments, I would usually feel like I needed a vigorous scrub in a scalding bath.

On one hand, I devoured respected authors who espouse a more traditional interpretation. I learned they preferred to be called "complementarians." In an honest attempt to be faithful to the text, complementarians teach that women must not be permitted to lead based solely on their gender. Many of these teachers sound almost apologetic—though there are some who summon maximum machismo and take rip-roaring delight in their pulpit-pounding defense of male supremacy.

However, from the more humble to the blatantly arrogant, the complementarians I studied all believed that their view rested upon a biblical foundation. They were convinced the Bible teaches that women were created to be the man's helper. Therefore, women are always supposed to be in a submissive, supportive, non-leadership role. And, obviously, they supported their case with the scripture passages that appear very prohibitory toward women.

I could see what they were saying.

Complementarians do not believe women are less valuable in personhood, but women are inescapably secondary in position. In their studied opinions, since the woman was meant by God's design to be man's lovely assistant, it is therefore unbiblical and wrong for a woman to lead or to teach men.

However, though I could see in Scripture much of what they argued, I was stumped by other scriptures which seem to declare just the opposite. For example, "In Christ there is no male and female" (Galatians 3:28). Or, that both "your sons and your daughters would prophesy" (Acts 2:17, quoting Joel 2:28). Not to mention the incongruous apostolic shout-outs Paul gave to several women serving on his ministry teams and in other leadership positions within the Church. Whenever I would read the more traditional authors, I knew their arguments did not ring true, but I couldn't put my finger on exactly what was false.

That was the complementarians, the traditionalists. On the other hand—and here we are again with those mixed feelings!—I would read the arguments from across the aisle, as it were. Vocal, sometimes shrill, denouncements of male supremacy from the opposing, pro-female side. And, though you would suppose, based on how my thinking had been trending, that I would have been readily susceptible to their arguments, I actually was not. Is that surprising? Maybe. But in my gut, again, I felt that something still was not right.

Sometimes the pro-women authors were hostile, even bitter over the way women had been mistreated by "The Patriarchy." Some feminist Bible scholars, both men and women, would dismiss Paul's words out of hand because they deemed that he just got it wrong. Some even went completely over the edge and wrote Paul off as overtly misogynist and guilty of distorting the equality-oriented gospel of Jesus into another gospel altogether.[3] Some made Paul the culprit.

Most, however, were quite committed to the inerrancy of Scripture. They took Paul seriously. They called themselves "egalitarians." They did not advocate male supremacy, and they stopped short of the extreme "cancel Paul" movement flourishing among far left Christian feminists. But, to my discomfort, some

---

[3] Misogyny is the "dislike of, contempt for, or ingrained prejudice against women." (New Oxford American Dictionary) Dictionary.com defines misogyny as "hatred, dislike, or mistrust of women, manifested in various forms such as physical intimidation and abuse, sexual harassment and rape, social shunning and ostracism, etc.; ingrained and institutionalized prejudice against women; sexism."

egalitarians still explained away the difficult verses. Many argued from various angles that the prohibition passages in Paul are not for us—they were only culturally relevant for Paul's day and time. Most pro-women advocates ended up in the same place: some portion of the Scriptures are not applicable today, without clear reasons as to why and how those passages don't apply.

That made me uncomfortable. Paul wrote two-thirds of the New Testament. If he got it wrong, or if his teachings were binding only for the early church, then why would God preserve his false ideas in the Bible? There are many pseudo-epigraphical and apocryphal writings from the early Christian period that Holy Spirit through the Church kept out of the canon of Scripture. Why include Paul's writings if they were so wrong? And how do we determine which portions are for us and which portions we can dismiss? Doesn't that become rather arbitrary?

That didn't work for me.

What Chaldee Means

On and on it went. Six years. *Six long years.* That's how long I had been embroiled in this inner struggle with neither side giving me satisfactory answers. Finally, while I was taking the Christian Leadership University class, light began to dawn.

And guess what I found out? I found out what *Chaldee* meant. It was one of the first things that I encountered in the course, and it became a revelation that fundamentally shifted everything. It demonstrated how the anti-woman bias was neither biblical nor godly. It also clarified how these discriminatory traditions became part of Jewish culture and legal system and made their way into the Christian New Testament.

Let me unpack it for you.

Back in the day, during the Jewish Exile into Babylon (which began in the late fifth century BC), the Jewish rabbis and scholars wrote down their oral traditions so they would not lose their Jewish culture while living in captivity in a foreign land. You may remember that Babylon was the region that Abraham had left when the Lord called him out of Ur of the Chaldeans, an ancient cultural center of the pagan world.

Abraham's Journey From Ur

Look at the map of ancient Mesopotamia, and you will see that Ur was located in the southern part of what became the Babylonian Empire where the mighty Euphrates and Tigris rivers flowed. And this region is exactly where the exiled Jews returned during the Babylonian Captivity. Fifteen centuries after Abraham left Ur, his descendants were ripped violently from their Promised Land and exiled back to the land Abraham originally left. Talk about coming full circle.

You have to wonder if Father God was giving Israel a do-over, a chance to retrace the steps of Abraham and get it right. And "getting it right" would have meant returning to the "steps of the faith of [their] father, Abraham" (Romans 4:12). It would have meant returning to faith. But Israel did not fully repent and return to faith. Instead, they turned to religion. Though Israel never returned to the idolatry that caused the Exile, yet the prophets make it clear that the Hebrews did not turn fully to the Lord with all their heart. Sadly, this meant that the seventy years of captivity were extended to seventy "weeks of years" (490 years). (See Daniel 10-12)

And it was during this Babylonian Captivity that the Jewish rabbis started developing and writing down the oral tradition. They believed that the oral law was given to Moses and handed down verbally through the generations. The rabbis believed that, by creating a codified tradition, they could unify the scattered exiles and preserve Jewish identity in a strange land.

That was a great plan, really. No matter where the Jewish people ended up geographically or into what society they assimilated, by preserving their traditions in writing, they would forever remain "Jewish." ("Hebrew" would be a more accurate word—the term "Jewish" was not used for many centuries after the Exile into Babylon, but for us "Jewish" is the common name for the Hebrew people throughout history. A little anachronism never hurt anybody.)

Throughout the Exile and later after the fall of Jerusalem in AD 70, the Jews preserved their identity and culture by rehearsing their past on religious holidays, by practicing their distinct culture in dress and customs and by training their children in separate Jewish schools to love Jewish rabbinic teachings. As *Fiddler On the Roof* so poignantly portrayed, "Trah-deeeee-shun" (can you hear Tevye singing?) was the glue that kept the Jews together.

It is amazing to me that the Jewish people never lost their identity even after generations of living outside their homeland. By rooting their identity in conformity to their distinctive customs, they could still be "Jewish" no matter where they lived. History later proved how vital this was to their survival as their nation without a homeland for nearly two thousand years. All because the Rabbis had the foresight to codify their oral tradition. Remarkable!

But the oral tradition had a dark side. Though the Jews remained distinct as a people in many ways, yet they were deeply influenced by the culture around them in other ways. Something was in the water, as it were. The spirit of Babylon permeated their mindsets, and their traditions were infected with pagan influence. In fact, the religion of the Jews during post-exilic period, often called "the Second Temple period," became so poisoned with the Babylonian spirit—the spirit of Babel, the attempt to reach the heavens through hierarchical human righteousness and religious works—that early Christians identified the religious system entrenched in the temple at Jerusalem prior to AD 70 as "mystery

Babylon" (Revelation 17:5). This "Babylonian spirit" is what Jesus opposed so fiercely during his earthly ministry.

The oral tradition was so influenced by Babylon, in fact, that one part of the Jewish Talmud—rabbinic commentaries on the Law and the traditions—was later called the "Babylonian Talmud." This is an explicit nod to the influence that the Exile in Babylon had on the Jewish religion.

I dug deeper.

Then I saw it. Not only was Jewish tradition shaped in the land of the Chaldeans, it was written down in the *language* of the Chaldeans. Which was—do you remember?—*Chaldee*. Talk about having a flashback: all I could see was that clipboard with "C-H-A-L-D-E-E" scrawled across the bottom.

As Riggs and Winer put it, "the language of the Talmud is commonly termed *Chaldee*."[4] *Chaldee* is Eastern Aramean, from the Babylon province occupying the Euphrates and Tigris river region.[5] This is the language the exiled Jews learned while being held captive to the world power that enslaved them.

But I still needed to connect "Chaldee" to the women's issue. Since the heart of all my research was

---

[4] Riggs, Elias DD, and Georg Benedikt Winer, *A Manual of the Chaldee Language*. (New York: Anson D.F. Randolf and Co., 1858), 13, note 2. See also John McClintock and James Strong, *Cyclopaedia of Biblical, Theological, and Ecclesiastical Literature, Vol II, C-D*, (New York: Harper & Brothers, 1894), 201

[5] Riggs, *A Manual of the Chaldee Language*, 9

about what "she has Chaldee" meant to the question of women in leadership, I probed deeper. I now knew that "Chaldee" was referring to the Jewish traditions shaped in the land of the Chaldeans and written in their language. But what exactly did this have to do with the women's issue?

It only took a bit for the last piece to fall into place. I started looking into what the rabbis had to say in their traditions about women. It didn't take long to find it; and when I did, I was stunned. Some of the most vitriolic, misogynistic opinions I had ever read emerged on my screen. It was breathtaking, but in a bad way.

> *Misogyny was systematized and woven into their daily life. Contempt became a daily discipline.*

The rabbis were not shy about it. Their contempt for women was brazen. They discussed their brutal treatment of women openly without shame. It was simply *how the world was for them.* They had no awareness of how anti-God and anti-heaven their views were. They reflected and amplified the views of Babylon without hesitation. It was their norm.

Bad move, Norm.

As the oral traditions were codified, misogyny was systematized and woven into their daily life. Contempt became a daily discipline. For example, Jewish males were taught to start their day by declaring, "Thank God that I was not born a Gentile, a woman or an ignoramus." In several strange (to us) passages, there is even an extended discussion about dropping the word "ignoramus" and replacing it with "slave." The obliviously pompous discussion points out the fact that men giving thanks that they were not born a slave would be needlessly repetitious since they had already expressed thanks for not being born a woman. Since females were already doomed from birth to a life of serving men, the men offering thanks that they were not born a slave would be redundant.

Of course, they were right: indeed, it would be redundant. But the most startling thing is that the discussion centered around avoiding "redundancy"—God forbid that we repeat ourselves!—rather than overturning the bizarre assumption that women were created for a lifetime of domestic slavery. How did men ever get to the place where their mothers, sisters and wives were treated with such brazen contempt?

Those who wanted to change the phrase won. Hurrah.

I think the most shocking thing about it all for me is that it is still a common practice for Orthodox Jewish men to begin the day by thanking God that they were "not born a Gentile, a woman, or a slave."[6] It absolutely floors me to think that many twenty-first century Jewish women still listen to their husbands and sons thanking God every morning that they were not born a woman.

---

6 https://www.myjewishlearning.com/article/three-blessings/ and https://www.huffingtonpost.com/ari-hart/should-i-thank-god-for-not-making-me-a-woman_b_3197422.html

Wonder what impact that has on the men's view of their wives and daughters? Wonder what impact it has on how the women see themselves?

Unbelievable.

Many of the Jewish anti-female traditions are similar to those we still see in some strict Muslim cultures. For example, Jewish women had to cover their heads, like a mourner. Girls were not allowed to be educated. In fact, some rabbis felt it would be better for the Torah (the first five books of the Bible) to be burned than for it to be taught to a woman. These ladies were relegated to domestic servitude.

In the ancient Jewish documents, there is even a remarkably unperturbed discussion among the rabbis about not allowing women to leave the house very often. They opined that women would receive greater glory by staying in a corner of the house. These women had to do whatever their husbands told them to do, and the husbands were encouraged to beat rebellious wives with a whip. The women had no right of divorce and no ability to support themselves and their children anywhere in that culture. Women were literally born into slavery.

Another egregious example is the Talmudic "Ten Curses of Eve," which includes, among other outrageous statements, "She stays in the home and does not show herself in public like a man"—or as an earlier version put it, she is "confined within a prison." And a woman must cover her head "like a mourner" because she "brought death upon all the inhabitants of the world."[7] There you go—Adam still blames Eve for the Fall.

All this sounds shocking to us, but it was the norm for them. And still is for many. Remember, these rabbinic anti-female traditions were recorded in the Talmud, a written commentary on the Oral Tradition. And the Talmud is one of the most highly esteemed Jewish writings still used all over the world to shape and serve Jewish devotion.

Let me be clear. I don't mean to show disrespect to the Jewish people and their ancient religious documents. The Talmud has been highly important for the preservation of the Jewish people and culture. It is vital, however, that we grasp a central fact: *many of these oral traditions took shape in Babylon—in the world outside God's Kingdom.* These ideas *do not* represent the heart of Father God for his daughters.

Chaldee Is A Cancer

After sifting through all this, I leaned back and processed what I'd read. There it was. Right in front of me. Some of the worst anti-women sentiments ever written were recorded in the ancient language of *Chaldee.* But what did this have to do with my dream?

Just this: God was driving home the point that Babylon represents the world outside His Kingdom, outside the Promised Land, a place where His people are once again enslaved. It was the same world that

---

[7] http://jewishbible.blogspot.com/2005/10/ten-curses-of-eve-unpublishable.html

Abraham, the honored father of our faith, was called to leave. Here's what Father God was saying to me: "Susan, the same ungodly system that once enslaved my people has again enslaved the hearts and minds of the modern Church."

The Church has been living through its own Babylonian Captivity. Even though these pagan, anti-female sentiments originated in Babylon—the wrong kingdom!—they were woven over the centuries into the fabric of Judeo-Christian culture. Dark, evil thoughts infiltrated and imprisoned God's women.

> **Bondage at any level is the antithesis of freedom.**

Misogyny has never been God's will. Contempt for women arose from the power struggles rooted in humanity's Fall. The power structures of the world's corrupt systems rested precariously on male supremacy. If creational equality was pursued, the fragile house of cards would come crashing down. The evil powers that gained dominion over humans in the Fall could only preserve that power by fomenting division and conflict between humans.

And the root of that division and conflict always starts between men and women. This is why satan was—and is!—so vested in keeping a male boot pressed firmly on the female neck. The enemy seduced mankind to crave power, domination and control over each other, even to the extreme perversity of enslaving one's own family.

Bondage at any level is the antithesis of freedom. It is the antithesis of love, and it is the antithesis of God's Kingdom. As Paul said, "Where the Spirit of the Lord is there is freedom" (2 Corinthians 3:17). Where evil reigns, freedom is suppressed.

Imagine how I felt when I first encountered all this. I sat stunned for moment as my brain worked feverishly to process what I'd read. As you might imagine, I did my homework. I wanted to confirm that what I'd read was true. And the more I studied, the more I knew that I'd just stumbled—and not by accident!—across the answer to the dream I'd wrestled with for years.

When it began to really sink in that these traditions had been formalized and codified in *Chaldee*—in the language of the world outside God's Kingdom and the exact word spoken to me in my dream before I even knew what it meant!—I began to weep. God had indeed clearly spoken in my dream. Now there was no longer any doubt whatsoever. The dream meant that Christian women had been poisoned by satan through traditions and doctrines which had been created in a world far outside the influence of our King.

When I considered all I had wrestled with since the "Why send Mary?" moment, and then measured that against what I had just learned about the Talmud and its Chaldean influence, the enigmatic phrase, "She has *Chaldee*," became clear. It meant the entire Church was infected with this poison that spread like a cancer, being perpetuated by those who were "teaching as doctrines the precepts of men" (Matthew 15:9).

(By the way, the word for "men" in Matthew 15:9 does not mean "male"; it means "human." It is the Greek word *"anthropos."* So many times we think the Bible is saying "males" when it is simply saying "humans." The "precepts of men" are commandments, directives, rules of conduct, and guides made from worldly, fleshly thinking as opposed to being precepts coming from God Himself.)[8]

Through that distressing dream, Holy Spirit was highlighting the distress of God Himself over these anti-female sentiments. They had come from the world outside God's Kingdom, not from God's Word. Misogyny is an evil cancer poisoning the human race, but most Christians are blind to it—just like the woman in my dream standing behind the counter wearing the white lab coat. She was completely oblivious that there is a catastrophic problem, even though the evidence was right in front of her. It was spelled out in huge, eye-catching letters: "C-H-A-L-D-E-E!" Still, she was oblivious, believing all was as it was supposed to be.

What happens to a body with cancer if the cancer goes unnoticed and untreated? The cancer eats away and destroys God's beautiful creation. That's what happened at first to human culture and then to the Church when she conformed to human culture.

How Did the Chaldee Cancer Get In the Church?

And that's what kept troubling me. Exactly how did the Chaldee cancer get into the Church? I could clearly see

---

[8] See also Mark 7:7 and Isaiah 29:13-14.

its roots in Jewish culture. But how did it get into the Church? And even more troubling, how did it get into Scripture? How did we end up with passages in the New Testament that resonate with the harsh echoes of the Talmud?

I glanced back over the New Testament to see if an explanation jumped off the page. I started seeing how much Jewish tradition influenced the first generation of believers. Jesus and the apostles took great pains to correct stowaway notions carried over from Judaism into Christianity. The first Christians were Jews. They were trained in the Law of Moses and the Traditions of the Fathers. They were, as every generation is, a product of their times.

> *After the surprising resurrection of Jesus, everything had to be recalibrated mentally and spiritually.*

After the surprising resurrection of Jesus—they didn't see that coming!—everything, and I mean *everything*, had to be recalibrated mentally and spiritually. First generation Christians were now wrestling with how to think since they were born again and the Kingdom of God had broken into the world, shattering the ancient Babylonian systems that had worked into Judaism and into the temple worship that anchored Israel's religion, political and social life. The entire New Testament is written to sort all that out.

The first century Church fussed over everything. Circumcision. Sabbath keeping. Mosaic food laws. Fellowship with Gentiles. Food offered to idols. Slavery. Immorality. Celibacy. Head coverings. Resurrection. The Second Coming.

And equality for women.

It should be no surprise that the women's issue was an issue in the first century. As we shall see, much of Paul's writing is his answer to these questions. And we shall also see that much of what Paul addressed was rooted in the Mishnaic traditions of the Jews that codified anti-women feelings.

In the first century, there were several religio-political parties within Judaism, and one of the most conservative among them was the Pharisees. The "scribes and Pharisees" figured prominently in many of the controversies and debates that swirled around Jesus' ministry.

The scribes and Pharisees highly revered the traditions and doctrines of men. In fact, scholars assert that some Pharisees believed that the Traditions of the Fathers were more binding than the Torah. They believed the traditions were given to Moses as "Oral Law" and was passed down through the generations to be codified in the Talmud.

So it's no wonder that the Babylonian misogyny worked its way into the traditions of the scribes and Pharisees. And subsequent generations even embellished the traditions a bit. For example, by Jesus' day, women were not permitted to speak in public, not even to their husbands—and especially not if he was a rabbi. If a woman was to pass by her husband in public, she was to remain silent. If she spoke to him publicly, that would dishonor him.

Can you imagine that? Women were not even allowed to speak to their own husbands in public!

Jesus forcefully rejected the Pharisees' veneration of tradition over the Word of God. He addressed it in his teachings, but he also simply demonstrated the love of the Father in the life He lived. He demonstrated daily how Father God feels about His daughters. As Jesus said, "When you've seen me, you've seen the Father" (John 14:9).

As Bill Johnson so eloquently sums it up, "Jesus is perfect theology." I love how Jesus graciously treated women despite the harsh culture of His day. In fact, both Jesus and Paul were revolutionary in their treatment of and teaching on women. For example: though Jesus never sinned, yet He violated the manmade customs of His day by chatting with the woman at the well. According to the cultural protocol of that time, she was not allowed to talk to men in public. But Jesus was the one who started the conversation. To compound the *"faux pas,"* the woman was a Samaritan, a mixed race hated by the Jews. Later, when His disciples returned from getting food, it was her gender that shocked them, not her ethnicity.

> *At this point His disciples came, and they were amazed that He had been speaking with a woman, yet*

no one said, "What do You seek?" or, "Why do You speak with her?" (John 4:27)

They could not believe Jesus was having a conversation with a woman. The disciples were shocked speechless. Scandalous!

If the protocol regarding women speaking with men in public had been divinely sanctioned, Jesus would have honored it and refused to speak with the Samaritan woman. But he did not. Why? Because He despised the traditions of men that superseded and contradicted His Father's Word.

In Matthew 15 and Mark 7, Jesus called out the scribes and Pharisees for elevating their traditions and doctrines over the Word of God. By doing this, they rendered God's Word null and void.

"And so you cancel the word of God in order to hand down your own tradition. And this is only one example among many others." (Mark 7:13 NLT).

"Making the word of God of no effect through your tradition which you have handed down." (Mark 7:13 NKJV).

(See also Matthew 15:1-9, and Mark 7:1-13.)

Mixing the Word of God with tradition is sort of like mixing water into your gasoline. Your car will stop dead in the middle of the street. Even the most pious and religious people of Jesus' day had unknowingly been mixing worldly, human precepts into God's doctrines, making them powerless. Their religious vehicle—the Pharisee-mobile!—had stalled.

Yet Pharisaism crept into the Church, and through it, Babylonian misogyny. The early Church was heavily influenced by Pharisaic Judaism. It took some heavy lifting by Paul and the apostles to heave-ho those ideas right out of the church. But they were never able to fully erase the sinful tendency of fallen man to seek domination over others, and male supremacy came back with a vengeance like a recurring cancer.

Then it got worse. As the Church spread throughout the Roman Empire, the Babylonian spirit flared back up. When the Church became institutionalized after the Edict of Milan in 313, it soon became terminally hierarchicalized. The impulse to consolidate power and gain preeminence corrupted the Church, and we drifted back into the old Babylonian spirit.

Chaldee Is A Global Pandemic

Tragically, the enculturated abuse of women was not confined to Judaism or Christianity. And neither was it confined to ancient times. It's happened everywhere, all the time. To varying degrees, the marginalization and abuse of women has been a global pandemic infecting all of humanity.

The Muslim religion also caught the anti-women virus, and throughout the Islamic world, women are still severely oppressed. In twenty-first century Islam, Muslim women of certain sects and in certain countries are not allowed to have a driver's license, be educated, uncover their head or go out in public without a male chaperone from their family.

In some of these places, the women are tortured horribly if they do not submit and obey the men like a slave. Severe beatings, mutilations and honor killings are still culturally accepted practices. Women are often abused and even murdered by their own fathers and husbands for being disobedient. In some cases, young girls who are raped are put to death by their own families to remove the shame from their family name.

In other parts of the world, like some overpopulated Asian nations, governments restrict the number of children each family can have. Infant girls frequently are murdered or abandoned so the family can make room for a male child. The males are more valuable socially and economically—specifically, they are more able than girls to help support their parents later in life. Many girls die because boys are "better."

All over the globe, even right here in America, human trafficking in the sex slave trade is alive and well. Hapless girls are overpowered, threatened with murder and sold into slavery for men to dominate and exploit them. At the root of this horrific practice is the same discriminatory belief, played out to the extreme, that men have the right to own and control women for their own self-serving desires.

Does this sound like heaven? Does this sound like the Kingdom? I think not.

It's a Babylonian spirit. It's *Chaldee*.

Honor Disclaimer

We need to spend a few more minutes talking about the reality we face today in the world around us. The Babylonian spirit is alive and well. But just before we do, let me add an "honor disclaimer"—a clarification of what I'm saying to prevent misunderstanding.

Christians who oppose women in leadership may object that all I've cited above is an extreme version of hatred for women that they do not endorse. And of course they are right. I don't mean to suggest that Christians who oppose women in ministry agree on any level with the hideous examples I've given. But I do think that it is valid to point out that these extreme examples are endemic to the world's system, and that Christian prohibitions of women in leadership grow out of this bitter root. The poison may be diluted, but it is poison nonetheless.

We must distinguish between the Word of God and our human traditions. In contrast with some feminist teachers, I believe strongly that Paul's writings sovereignly included in the Bible are to be revered as Scripture. The Talmud and other oral traditions are not the inspired word of God. They are man's precepts. Some are wonderful; some are in error. In contrast, Paul's writings in the New Testament are never in error. They are the inspired Word of God.

Please do not confuse what I'm saying: the Bible, and what Paul says in it, is Holy Scripture and should be revered as such. The Bible is God's Word. It is one hundred percent accurate, and we can trust it implicitly. It is our plumb line. The Word of God is without error.

However, our human interpretation of Scripture is not. And that's where we often get off track. As we deal in this series with each of the difficult, seemingly female-restrictive verses in the Bible, that's what you'll see—our interpretation is what went wrong, not Paul's teaching.

What you will learn will blow you away. How this all fits together is earth-shattering. It is amazing. I promise, whether you are male or female, you will be liberated. The truth about God's Kingdom and how we all, male and female, fit into it will revolutionize your life.

The women's issue is key because the Church has been poisoned with *Chaldee*. Poisoned! The whole Church is sick, not just the females. When women are held in bondage, the entire body, including the men, is in bondage too. Misogyny is a cancer that has kept the Bride under satan's influence. If one half of a couple's glory is veiled, or half of their power restricted, then neither of them can function properly. *The effects are exponential!*

> *All of creation is still waiting for us to grow up and become who and what God created and designed us to be.*

If you have a car and half of it is broken, how well does the other half operate? Does it operate at half capacity? No! At best, it may creep along, but more likely it would be dead in a junkyard. It is one car. You cannot expect it to operate if half of it is broken. That is not how it was designed to work. That is not how we were designed either.

Male and female were created to be different parts of one powerful unit. Yet the world has not seen such a powerful, unified team walk the earth, at least not since the Garden. All of creation is still waiting for us to grow up and become who and what God created and designed us to be.

> *"For the anxious longing of the creation waits eagerly for the revealing of the sons of God"* (Romans 8:19).

(I'm sure you guessed as much, but "son" (*huios*) in this verse does not exclusively mean "male" child. The word can be used for boys, but it can also include girls. In context, the word refers to us becoming mature children as opposed to babies.)

The world is waiting for believers to mature, to grow up enough to take our rightful place and to destroy the enemy's evil domination over the world's systems. Since the Fall, we have forgotten who we truly are. The entire creation suffers as it waits for us to wake up out of our confusion. How creation longs for us to comprehend and lay hold of all that we are in Christ!

Can you see now why the Church is weak and less influential than She should be? She is broken. She is sick. She has *Chaldee*. She has been poisoned by unbiblical, worldly and incorrect beliefs. It is time for things to change. God is clearly at work bringing healing to the Body with His message of freedom for women, which will empower the men even more. *It's time for a Christian women's liberation movement!*

CHAPTER 5

WOMEN'S LIB

M isogyny did not start with the Talmud. And the language of anti-female sentiment is much older than *Chaldee*. The sin of prejudice against women is as old as sin itself. It all started in the Fall of man—and *woman*. It started in the curse, of course.

> *Your desire will be for your husband, and he will rule over you." (Genesis 3:16)*

Jesus came to break the curse. And part of breaking that curse included liberating women *as women*. Not just as humans, but as females. The curse upon women was much greater than just personal sin. As we noted above, women were forced by many men to carry the guilt for *all* sin, for women were judged to be the source of original sin.

Women throughout history were treated as contaminated creatures. Impure and beguiling. Poor men the world over were constantly led astray by those devious women. Not only did Jesus come to break the curse of individual sin, but He also came to break the curse of collective shame placed upon women by male-dominated culture.

Women's Liberation

Jesus came "to set free those who are oppressed" (Luke 4:18). No one fits that bill more than women. Jesus came to set the captives free. And no one was more captive than women. Jesus came to *liberate* women. He was the first "women's libber."

Don't jerk a knee, now.

I know that "Women's Lib" is a controversial term, but just hear me out. One of satan's most successful schemes is to bury a righteous cause under a pile of unrighteous red herrings. (Pretty fishy.) The liberation of women is the Lord's work. Yet the cause has been politicized and radicalized—in fact, it's been hijacked!—by people with an extreme agenda, and those who oppose women's liberation as a threat to the status quo use that fact to discredit the entire agenda. But to discredit the liberation of women is to discredit the agenda of the Great Liberator himself, King Jesus.

One of the most astonishing ironies of the battle for women's liberation is that traditionalist Christians end up joining forces with Christ's enemies to prevent women from being restored to their original creational position alongside men. Satan opposes equality because his strategy for world domination is "divide and conquer." Traditionalists oppose liberation because of mistaken interpretations of Scripture that seem to require female subjugation. And due to that honest but deadly mistaken, sincere Christians find themselves, like James and John, operating inadvertently from the wrong spirit. (Luke 9:55)

It is true that the Women's Liberation Movement has been aligned in popular perception with the sexual revolution and abortion rights. Satan has successfully deceived so many women into believing that their greatest empowerment lies in their right to sleep with whomever they wish and to decide when impregnated if their unborn child lives or dies. What a tragic lie!

However, popular perception notwithstanding, most women in the Women's Liberation Movement are not anti-family, anti-Christ and anti-Bible. There are countless millions of women who have fought a quiet struggle for equality in households, offices and factories everywhere. They have contended valiantly for better treatment and fair

> *So, to avoid being maligned, many faithful, believing women have either fought for liberation under the radar or stayed safely on the margins of the fight until others gained the ground for them.*

wages, for a voice in leadership and a clear, unobstructed path to career advancement. They have pushed back relentlessly against pervasive sexual harassment and refused to be reduced to sexual objects for the pleasure of ogling men.

Yet, for whatever reason, some label all women who contend for liberation as "Jezebels." Jezebel, you may recall from your Sunday School days, was an evil queen in the Bible who fought against God and his prophet, Elijah. Jezebel stands in history as the epitome of a manipulative, controlling, vindictive woman. If you are a Jezebel, then obviously you are a horrible person.

That kind of woman.

A woman who becomes too strong or bucks the status quo is forced to fight off this insulting label. And, as a God-loving, Bible-honoring woman, who would want to be called *that?* So, to avoid being maligned, many faithful, believing women have either fought for liberation under the radar or stayed safely on the margins of the fight until others gained the ground for them.

Biblical Feminism?

Think about the stigma that goes with being called a "feminist." I used to shrink back from identifying myself as a "feminist" because I had this narrow idea that all feminists were *female supremacists,* which some are. But I most decidedly was *not,* and I found out that most feminists are not either.

The media-driven image of the male-hating, bra-burning, marriage-loathing "feminist" is an unfair caricature carefully crafted by the enemy to push his agenda from the opposite extremes of radical feminism and conservative traditionalism. Remember, both ends of the political spectrum conspire inadvertently to prevent women from experiencing creational liberation.

I had to re-learn what feminism even means. Here's a good definition of feminism:

> "The doctrine advocating social, political, and all rights of women equal to those of men," and then by

extension, the "organized movement for the attainment of such rights for women."[1]

Due to the advances made with equal rights for men and women, most people would readily agree that this sort of "feminism" is desirable. However, most complementarians, though they are for the kind treatment of women, would not agree that this sort of "social, political" equality is desirable. They believe women are equal in their humanity, but never equal in their role. Complementarians believe that God created men to lead and women to follow. Period. So to them, women being equal socially and politically would violate the nature of creation. Complementarianism is extreme anti-feminism, but with a sweet, benevolent tone.

Of course, there are extremists within the pro-feminism side, as is true with every movement. And they seem to take up all the oxygen. If we are to have a evening news feature about women's issues, the media will nearly always invite on the show a woman who represents the farthest left edge, most likely a professor from a Gender Studies program that, truthfully, doesn't represent the vast majority of women. And most women sit watching bug-eyed, wondering where the heck the TV producer found this bizarre female specimen that claims to speak for us all.

For sure, there are angry, female-supremacists out there, and they all seem to have thousand watt megaphones. However, most feminists are neither anti-

<hr>

[1] https://www.dictionary.com/browse/feminism

family nor anti-male. Rather—and get this!—they are anti-discrimination. They are people that usually happen to be female and believe in the equality of men and women. And they are willing to stand up for it. And why not? Shouldn't we all stand up for what we believe in?

In fact, many feminists are men. Men who advocate for equality for men and women are some of the most effective feminists on the planet. As we shall see in the next chapter, the move of God that is working throughout the nations to restore creational equality is exploding throughout the ranks of God-fearing, truth-loving men. The hearts of men are turning! And when both men and women find unity on the women's issue, then, and only then, can the Church model and mediate unity to the nations.

I remember hearing about feminists being called "femi-Nazis," a term apparently made popular by a national radio personality. Everyone laughed it off as harmless shock-jock satire, but the damage was done. The negative stereotype of feminists was painfully reinforced. Who wants to be lumped in with Hitler and Co.?

That sort of popular mischaracterization has a chilling effect. So many Christian women fear being labeled negatively that they just lay low and keep quiet. Play dumb and maybe no one will know. How long have women been doing that? And this *really* matters because the fear of feminism in the Church has inadvertently given that contagious, cancerous *Chaldee* spirit permission to remain locked in, corrupting one more generation of young men and women. And by relegating half of the Body of Christ to subordination, the Church of Jesus is anemic, weak and broken.

That's why it matters.

Let me put it bluntly, just in case I've not been clear enough so far: the *Chaldee cancer* is a "doctrine of demons" (1 Timothy 4:1). The idea that women must be subordinate to men did not come from how God made the world. This idea is an illness that has infected the Church at a rate almost too massive to comprehend. The Church was intended to be a countercultural force for world transformation, but we have instead conformed generation after generation to the world's penchant for male supremacy.

> *The doctrine that women were created by God's design for a subservient role to men is a lie of the enemy, a lie cleverly crafted to divide and disempower humans.*

The doctrine that women were created by God's design for a subservient role to men is a lie of the enemy, a lie cleverly crafted to divide and disempower humans. How many women over the centuries have been prisoners in their own homes because they thought that is what God created them to do? Females were conditioned to believe that God created them to have kids and serve their husbands. And, of course, He *did*. But not *only*. For that matter, God also created men to have kids and serve their wives. Do you see that? Both men and women were created for family, work and worship.

Women's Liberation In History

Think about it with me for a minute. I wonder how many women have been born into slavery since the Fall of humans in the garden? *Almost all of them.* And I am *not* exaggerating for effect. While there were some societies throughout history where women enjoyed significant freedoms, most did not.

For example, it wasn't until the late 1800s in America that women at large gained the right to be educated and were allowed to own property. Think about how utterly *crippling* that is. If you cannot learn and you cannot own property, then you will always be at the mercy of those who can.

The pernicious doctrine of "coverture" is a shocking example of what I'm talking about. Ever heard of it? Neither had I. But here it is:

> Under the common law legal doctrine known as coverture, a married woman in Great Britain's North American colonies and later in the United States had hardly any legal existence apart from her husband. Her rights and obligations were subsumed under his. She could not own property, enter into contracts, or earn a salary. Over several decades, beginning in 1839, statutes that enabled women to control real and personal property, participate in contracts and lawsuits, inherit independently of their husbands, work for a

salary, and write [their own] wills, were enacted. Usually, concerns for family integrity and protecting a household from economic crisis, rather than a liberal conception of the role of women in society, motivated these changes.

Change came in piecemeal fashion. As late as 1867 a decision of the Supreme Court of Illinois in Cole v. Van Riper noted that, "It is simply impossible that a married woman should be able to control and enjoy her property as if she were sole, without practically leaving her at liberty to annul the marriage." [How sad is that perspective?—the author's un-suppress-able comment, sorry!] According to one analysis, the legislation came in three phases—allowing married women to own property, then to keep their own income, then to engage in business—and advanced more quickly in the West, exactly like female suffrage did.[2]

Does that even sound possible? Yet that's the world our great-grandmothers grew up in. Here's more.

By the late 1800s, women were slowly gaining the privileges of owning property, earning wages, and being allowed to enter into contracts, but there was still another major barrier. How could they do anything of those things well without good education? "Girls were usually taught how to read but not how to write

---

[2] https://en.wikipedia.org/wiki/
Married_Women%27s_Property_Acts_in_the_United_States

in early America."[3] Most all higher education was traditionally closed to women because they were believed to be intellectually inferior and because it was feared that education would not properly prepare them for their "natural role" of wife and mother.[4] Throughout the years, and in most all countries, women had to fight for the right to be educated.

The liberation of women was near-impossible without female education. But the men who held the power to approve or disapprove female education had to be persuaded that educating women would improve their performance at home. This, then, became the bargaining chip for advocates of female education: the women assured the men that they would pursue higher learning and still faithfully perform their duties at home.

"A lot of people compromised by saying that better educated women made better mothers and wives; it's been a pretty standard defense over the centuries."[5]

If the women pinky-promised that they would still do all the housework and take care of the kids, then the magnanimous men agreed that those silly women could learn about other things too—like reading, writing,

---

[3] https://www.americanboard.org/blog/11-facts-about-the-history-of-education-in-america/

[4] https://www.bustle.com/p/heres-how-women-fought-for-the-right-to-be-educated-throughout-history-53150

[5] *Ibid.*

arithmetic, history, science and art. So long as no one threatened the power structure built to serve male supremacy. As long as The Powers That Be were not asked to downgrade their superior status nor take on increased responsibilities, then women earned the right to be educated.

Isn't that touching?

As the status of women was slowly coming up in the world, other deep, systemic changes began to take place, changes that signaled real, substantive progress. For example, in 1910, Congress passed the White-Slave Traffic Act and the Mann Act, both of which outlawed the kidnapping of females and transporting them across state lines to work as sex slaves. We hear a lot about human trafficking these days, but can you imagine what it must have been like when women were regarded as nothing more than property owned by men for their pleasure and amusement.

Thankfully, more than a hundred years ago, sex trafficking finally provoked enough national outrage for Congress to pass laws designed specifically to protect vulnerable women.[6] More than a hundred years after our nation's founding, and more than forty-five years after enslaved people were emancipated. But better late than never, I guess.

However, what truly turned the world upside down was World War I, which shook the nations from

6 https://en.wikipedia.org/wiki/
History_of_sexual_slavery_in_the_United_States and https://
en.wikipedia.org/wiki/Mann_Act

1914-1918. As millions of men from around the globe were shipped off to war, millions of women entered the workforce. They had to do so to keep their families and their countries alive. Prior to the war, many women worked in the textile factories or domestic-type jobs, jobs that were considered women's work. But after the war broke out, millions of women all over the world stepped into men's jobs.

Of course, these jobs were not yet a sign of permanent female advancement toward equality, for the vast majority of working women were simply filling the jobs that had been vacated by the men. The men were coming home, and they would want their jobs back.

Women also worked with the Army. Females could not officially serve in the military, but they could serve the soldiers as nurses and cooks, and many did. Women also went into the fast-growing munitions factories building weapons for the war effort. Conditions were often harsh, and they were paid much less than their male counterparts. But it was a start. The barriers that had previously kept women out of the male-dominated workplaces started breaking down out of sheer necessity.[7]

Think about how much the world shifted right after World War I. In 1920, only two years after the Armistice, women in America finally won the right to vote. Countless suffragists had been fighting relentlessly for over half a century for the right of women to vote. But

---

[7] http://www.striking-women.org/module/women-and-work/world-war-i-1914-1918

those in power had always refused to grant women the franchise. The idea of male and female equality was still seen as absolutely preposterous, but women in general had gained enough power and respect that they could go to the polls and vote.

That's pretty staggering when you think about it.

Now the female opinion would count on Election Day. *Progress!*

Where Are We Now?

I need to pause for a moment. As I read back through the sections above, it is so hard for me to even fathom the world in which our female ancestors lived, worked and dreamed. Women were not fundamentally different, biologically or spiritually, than they are now. They were born as beautiful little girls with dreams, hopes and aspirations. They longed to be active, successful and fulfilled, just as all humans do. But their dreams were cut short, their hopes dashed to the ground. They were given only one path to happiness: indentured servitude as a wife and mother. And while marriage and motherhood is a source of deep joy for women, it is not *the only thing women were created to do.*

> *While marriage and motherhood is a source of deep joy for women, it is not the only thing women were created to do.*

It is even more difficult for me to fathom what they lived through when I consider how much freedom I have enjoyed, even through all my "mixed feelings." Though I've struggled to sort out my role as a woman, especially in the church, I have lived a life of such amazing freedom in comparison to my female forebears.

I mentioned that 1920 was when women gained the right to vote. It's pretty hard to comprehend that it was only one hundred short years ago. We just passed the centennial. That's pretty astonishing. Yet I know freedom is never free, and I am so thankful to those formidable women who paid such a high price for the precious liberty I now sometimes take for granted. I get a say in the future of our country. How extraordinary is that! And yet the most extraordinary thing is that such an ordinary human right should be considered extraordinary at all.

A century later, how are we doing? Most Judeo-Christian families hold their wives and mom's in high esteem. Things are certainly far better than in millennia past where hapless women were tossed around like prized possessions. However, even in the twenty-first century, where we congratulate ourselves on being such an advanced society, men and women are still not usually equal partners in life.

In most families, the husband is still "head of household." And, even though that archaic language has mostly disappeared from society at large, the average family still adheres to the ancient power structures engrained in human history. It's in our DNA, it seems.

Ask a stranger on the street what "the head of the house" means, and nearly all will answer, "The Boss." And even in homes where both the husband and wife would vigorously assure us that they share power, there is still a subconscious bias toward men leading and women going along. Some of that may arise naturally from the physical dominance of men—their (usually) larger size, deeper voice and greater strength—but much of it comes from cultural conditioning.

And, as counterintuitive proof for my argument, in the families where women say they share equal power that power is often expressed as passive aggressive manipulation and control. The woman's need to get her way is expressed underhandedly because that's how generations of women before her learned to cope with being powerless. All that simply proves what I'm saying: equality between men and women is still elusive.

Oddly enough, this imbalance persists even in secular society, which doesn't share the Christian necessity to align behavior with Scripture. Though gender discrimination may be less obvious in the world, the notion lives on that females have the primary responsibility for domestic duties for no other reason than her gender. That is still deeply entrenched in our collective psyche.

For example, I recently had two male clients openly assert that the dishes are the woman's job. I am a real estate broker and love helping people navigate the home buying and home selling process.[8] And in the course of my work, I often get a glimpse into how families think. You would be amazed at what gets shared inadvertently when people are searching for the perfect home.

First story. I was recently showing homes to a young, millennial couple. We were looking at older, smaller homes that would fit within their budget. In one of the homes, I pointed out that the kitchen did not have space for a dishwasher to be installed. The husband jokingly grabbed his wife's wrist and lifted her arm up high, like a boxing referee would do with a champion who just won the match. "Here's our dishwasher," he said with a big smile. Of course, he meant it affectionately, so proud in an innocent, sweet way. He honestly meant her no disrespect.

It's not really about respect though. It's more about the assumptions that drove his mental reflexes. This young man was genuinely happy to be married, loved his wife and kids madly. But without hesitation, when the dishes came up his assumptions jumped immediately to *the woman* being the domestic one. He was most likely raised that way and fully unaware that it was awkward for her.

The young woman smiled hesitantly. She seemed torn between her affection for the man she deeply loved, knowing that he was just being silly, and the low-level

---

[8] Dewbrew Realty, Inc. serves the Fort Worth and Dallas, TX metroplex and surrounding areas. We would be happy to serve you here, or we can find a great agent referral for you anywhere in America. www.dewbrewrealty.com, Team@DewbrewRealty.com, 817-807-2246

insult that the joke implied. And she had probably been the "chief cook and bottle washer" since day one in their marriage. She apparently accepted without protest that the dishes were her responsibility even though she also worked outside the home. So, while his joke was harmless on one level, on another level it reflected generations of suppression.

Second story. A few weeks later, I was showing homes to another gentleman. He was about twenty years older than the first guy. We were viewing homes with his mother and step-father. In one of the homes the step-dad pointed out that there was no dishwasher in the kitchen. The man didn't miss a beat: "That's okay, I have a girlfriend."

I blanched. Trust me, I tried so hard to retract my bugging eyes, force a plastic smile and freeze my best poker face in place. It didn't work. I couldn't hide that fact that my heart was breaking. It wasn't really about who washes the dishes. It was just so indicative of the devaluing of women that the world has enculturated since the Fall. I am not being overly dramatic either. I really do see this as epic spiritual warfare on which rests the fate of humanity. And there's not one ounce of hyperbole in any of that. I mean it.

The gentleman must have seen the parade of emotions stamping across my face. He looked at me for a long second or two, and then added, "Or I can just buy paper." As if that fixed it. All nice and tidy.

Obviously, he believes dishwashing is a female's job. Only two options presented themselves to his mind:

One, either his girlfriend could get her butt over here and do her job; or, two, he could buy disposable products and chunk everything in the trash when done. The one single idea that *never crossed his mind* was that *he* could wash the dishes. It simply never occurred to him.

Now, I know that multitudes of men wash the dishes every night. *This is not about the global stats on dishwashing.* This is about the underlying assumptions regarding domestic tasks that expose deeper assumptions about gender roles. Dishes are a minuscule part of our daily chores. Life is much more than dishes. But I am using such a simple domestic task to demonstrate a pervasive mindset that persists in our culture.

Here's an even more shocking example to prove my point. A friend recently told me a story about a mom— and a Christian mom, at that!—who asked her overgrown teenage son to do a chore in the house. Just some random chore. Nothing big. The teen's response shocked me. He replied dismissively,

"I don't have to do that because I don't have a vagina."

What?! Say that again? No, actually, don't. I can't believe he said it the first time.

His astonishing response was profoundly disrespectful, to his mom and to women everywhere. But the young knucklehead believed he was in the right. As a young, Christian male growing up in modern-day America, he felt completely comfortable reducing women down to strange little people with vaginas who are on the planet to serve men. Astonishing.

Does that feel Christlike to you? Me either.

But the gender-role-assumption train runs both ways on the track. On the flip side, culture has created another set of assumptions for men. Most Christian women expect their men to take on all the financial and heavier responsibilities of life. They believe it is a man's job to be the bread-winner, the provider.

This creates its own set of problems. Instead of seeing themselves as true equal partners, they view the husband as responsible for everything, The Fixer who makes everything better. This makes the man the one at fault for everything wrong in the woman's life. If only he was a better leader, a better dad, a better husband, a better whatever, then they wouldn't have the problems they face.

> God is preparing us for greater Kingdom glory. Life is training for reigning.

This is tragically evident more among Christian women who have been trained to believe that their husbands are their head. They often muse that if their men were more spiritual or had more faith, then their family would not have the problems they have. In their mind, since the man is the head, the buck stops with him —and that means that it's his fault when life isn't perfect.

How wrong is that?! In this life, as Jesus said, we all have tribulation, period. (John 16:33) It's not necessarily because the husband is a lousy head. It may mean that God is preparing us for greater Kingdom glory. Life is training for reigning. There will always be battles to face and win. This life is not about seeing how comfortable and trouble-free your man can make you.

All these gender-specific stereotypes inevitably create resentment on both sides. She will hate doing chores forced on her by being born female. Especially when she works as hard as he does 9-5. And he will resent her and those insatiably hungry kids for spending all his money that he busts his butt to earn. He will feel like he can never produce enough to keep her happy.

If we practiced open communication and learned how to make mutual decisions throughout the shifting seasons of life, and if we did so with a ready willingness on both sides to surrender all to each other, then those resentments would melt away. Both husbands and wives must identify their ingrained assumptions and prejudices as they navigate these all important discussions. It's not always true that the female will do a better job with the child after they are weaned. And it's no longer an absolute fact that the male, simply because of his gender, will make more money for the family.

It is true that only a female can give birth or nurse an infant. But it's not true that men are incapable of taking care of children, cooking and cleaning. They are not physically or psychologically unable. Rather, they have been conditioned and trained that way—by us. By you and me and generations of parents and grandparents. Male supremacy is woven into the warp and woof of societal fabric. We can't expect to snap our fingers and everything change. We must be intentional about long, slow transformation.

In most of the families I know, it is still expected that household duties are the primary responsibility of the female—simply because she's female. Even if you have a good man who helps around the house, the responsibility for domestic chores in most American households falls to those with female anatomy, regardless of what other responsibilities they carry.

Now, remember we are talking about domestic roles because it is the most real-world example that proves how ingrained our assumptions of male superiority really are. So think a bit further with me.

CHAPTER 6

MIND THE GAP

In 1837, Oberlin College in Ohio was the first college in America to admit female students. Progress, indeed. It was many decades later before other, male-only schools would open to women. Several women-only colleges opened between the 1860s and 1890s, but all other male-only colleges remained closed to women for a long while after Oberlin opened up. Oberlin was way ahead of the times.

Yet Oberlin opened to women with a huge caveat.

"In addition to studying, the women have to do laundry and cook meals for the male students."[1]

From my twenty-first century vantage point, my initial response to that is, "You've got to be kidding, right?" I mean, I could see this being done on Saturday Night Live, but not in real life, surely. And yet it was real life, especially for the girls who lived it. The underlying belief system was that domestic chores are inherently "women's work," and that females were created to serve males. The women had to earn the right just to be in the building by serving the men—and by doing so with appropriate gratitude for the privilege.

---

[1] https://www.factmonster.com/people/women-influence/firsts-american-womens-history

You may wonder if traces of this mindset still exist. Let's take a look and see.

We spoke earlier about 1920 and the right to vote being granted to women. Next, the Roaring Twenties gave way to the Great Depression. Then came World War II (1939-1945), and that was a total game changer. Just like World War I, World War II recalibrated American society, but this time more permanently.[2] Prior to World War II, most women who worked in the workforce were expected to return to homemaking when they got married. Following the Second World War, things were different:

> Despite the stereotype of the "1950s housewife," by 1950 about 32% of women were working outside the home, and of those, about half were married. World War II had solidified the notion that women were in the workforce to stay.[3]

In the post-war era, as female employment became a more regular feature of American society, women started pushing for equal opportunities and for equal pay for the same job. We made really great strides forward in the 1960s and 1970s. Women were no longer relegated to domestic service industries and factories, which they had been grudgingly permitted by men to do since these jobs were much like the domestic tasks done by women in the home. Sort of, "Let her work, Fred, but

---

[2] https://www.khanacademy.org/humanities/us-history/rise-to-world-power/us-wwii/a/american-women-and-world-war-ii

[3] *Ibid.*

make sure she still doesn't get out of her place." But by the 1960s even Fred couldn't stop the inevitable: women were gaining employment equality.

In fact, the momentum gained such traction that by 1963, Congress passed the Equal Pay Act making it illegal to pay different rates to men and women for the same work. The next year, in 1964, the Equal Rights Act made it illegal for employers to discriminate based on race or sex. "Never before had it been illegal for a company to refuse to hire or promote a woman just because of her sex."[4] Gender discrimination became illegal the year I was born.

You can thank me later.

During the 1980s, female wages rose from sixty cents to seventy-two cents for every dollar a man made in the same position. As of 2010, according to that US Census, we had moved that needle up to eighty-one cents on the dollar.[5]

That's progress, but there's still a significant gap, often called the "pay gap," or "wage gap." These days, women still have to work two more months a year to earn the same amount as a man in the same position. Of course, these are averages, but it is still sobering.

What is most striking is that the gap is narrower for lower income jobs and and wider for top paying jobs. Women earn up to eighty-eight percent of what a man

[4] https://www.factmonster.com/people/women-influence/firsts-american-womens-history

[5] https://www.dol.gov/wb/factsheets/Qf-laborforce-10.htm

earns in the lower income sectors, but only about seventy-four percent at the top jobs. In today's world, the gender wage gap widens the higher up the ladder you go.[6]

However, the reason behind the gender wage gap is not simply prejudice or anatomy. It is important to look at these numbers with a broader perspective in mind. In today's modern, secular world, most companies aren't paying women less just because they are female. Sure, there are some companies where "good-ol'-boys" still manage their companies like that. But, by and large, men in corporate America are not anti-female like they were in generations past. Rather, there is a diversity of reasons why the gender pay gap still exists.

> *By and large, men in corporate America are not anti-female like they were in generations past. Rather, there is a diversity of reasons why the gender pay gap still exists.*

Countless studies have been done on the gender pay gap, but allow me for a moment to summarize the top reasons for pay disparity as I see it. Remember, we're talking about all this to expose the *Chaldee* spirit that has infected all of human society, particularly the Church.

---

6 https://www.pbs.org/newshour/economy/analysis-women-continue-make-less-men

In my opinion, here are the top three reasons:

Reason One:

Women gravitate toward lower paying jobs like nursing and teaching at much higher percentages than men. Why do they do that? Because, statistically, more women than men are attracted to jobs that serve people directly. Not all, of course, but a greater percentage of women want to work in relationally-based jobs. For many women, it is simply more rewarding.

Females tend to be more interested in people than things.[7] Since jobs that focus on relational service and take care of one person or one small group of people at a time cannot be mass produced, the jobs produce less revenue. It's simple economics. People in these jobs, most often women, earn less money.

The prevailing choice among women to work in relational jobs is often a result of an inherent desire among females to nurture, but—let's face the reality— much of this tendency is also driven by culturally conditioned expectations. Women have been taught for millennia that females were created for supportive roles rather than leadership roles. This conditioning has inevitably influenced female employment choices for generations. As women entered the workforce this past century, it was initially far more acceptable to be a nurse or a secretary. It was better for everyone if the girl

---

[7] https://www.washingtonexaminer.com/opinion/jordan-peterson-is-here-to-explain-the-gender-pay-gap-to-the-media

served as the assistant rather than the boss, particularly over men.

Female bosses were often contemptuously labeled as "butch." Women who were too strong were rejected as unattractive and unfeminine. That's no fun. (Which girls reportedly want to have.) No one wants to go to work day after day and wade through all that. So women just adapted. That multi-generational adaptation created a pattern among women of choosing jobs that align more with perceived female characteristics, and those jobs by their nature usually pay less. Voila, wage gap.

Reason Two:

Most women, at least those in my age group, grew up believing that it is the man's responsibility to provide financially for the family. If you grew up in religious circles, then this was most likely intensified by religious teaching that sacralized cultural norms as God's will. Even the irreligious, like my dad, reinforced these religious norms because they were raised that way, even though they long ago forsook meaningful devotion to Christ.

So when young girls dream of their future, their expectation is already bent toward careers that do not earn enough to provide for their family. That's the guys' job! (Sorry, guys! We heaped on you way more "bread-winner" pressure than you were supposed to carry.)

Then, these sanguine young ladies are stunned later in life when they smash head-on into a brick wall of reality: nearly half will be single moms and the sole breadwinner, and the other almost half will need to provide a second income for the family to survive.

There are exceptions, but that's the brutal reality for most. And what do they do now? They were simply not prepared for this. So they end up taking whatever jobs they can get, and the whatever-you-can-get-jobs are not usually well-paid.

Reason Three:

Reason number three is all about children. Jordan Peterson argues,

> The real pay gap is between mothers and fathers, not between women and men. Just this year, in fact, the National Bureau of Economic Research published a study that showed the gender gap "can be attributed to the dynamic effects of children."[8]

Here's the reality: most women today still take on the primary responsibility for caring for their children. No doubt this is somewhat attributed to biology, to the fact that women give birth and nurse children in their infancy. But there's no doubt that this expectation is driven by culture as well.

This means, when you do the child-bearing, child-caring math, women in the workplace who choose to have children will tend to make less than men. It's simply a matter of time—literally. Women who have

[8] https://www.washingtonexaminer.com/opinion/jordan-peterson-is-here-to-explain-the-gender-pay-gap-to-the-media

children work fewer hours in the week and fewer years in their life. That translates into lower average pay.

For example, many top-level female executives take off more hours or days than men for childcare reasons. Mothers are far more likely to leave their job for weeks or even months when they give birth. Many women choose to leave their career altogether to stay at home with the children, at least while the kids are young. All of this factors in the overall gender pay comparison statistics.

That, as I see it, are the three reasons for the wage gap. No doubt, there are other relevant factors, but I see these three as most influential. As you can see—and this is hugely important to my *Chaldee cancer* argument at the center of this book—the gender wage gap is not directly, or even mostly, attributable to overt male chauvinism.

> **The gender wage gap is not directly, or even mostly, attributable to overt male chauvinism.**

There are other, more indirect, culturally-conditioned factors at play here.

Want more stats? Here you go.

- More than five decades after the Equal Rights Act was passed to prevent discrimination, single moms are still twice as likely to be in poverty as single dads (forty-three percent of single moms and twenty-four percent of single dads live below the poverty line).[9]

- Women make up more than fifty percent of the population,[10] but hold only a little more than twenty percent of the seats in Congress.[11]

- Women make up nearly half the workforce, but only six percent of Fortune 500 companies (or their equivalent worldwide) are led by women.[12]

- Graduates of law and business schools tend to earn equivalent wages immediately after graduation, but diverge widely as they progress in their careers. Studies show that by fifteen years after graduation, male lawyers earned fifty-two percent more than their female counterparts and male MBA graduates earned eighty-two percent more between ten and sixteen years out of school.[13]

Crazy stats, huh?!

Now, get what I'm saying: this is not because of legislation preventing women from leading. It is not

9 https://www.usatoday.com/story/tech/news/2017/03/29/sheryl-sandberg-interview-lean-in-four-years-later/99749464/

10 https://www.census.gov/quickfacts/fact/table/US/LFE046216

11 http://www.cawp.rutgers.edu/women-us-congress-20186

12 https://www.usatoday.com/story/tech/news/2017/03/29/sheryl-sandberg-interview-lean-in-four-years-later/99749464/

13 https://www.pbs.org/newshour/economy/analysis-women-continue-make-less-men

because repressive males are holding women back. In fact, corporations and lawmakers aggressively seek women to lead due to widespread cultural pressure to be inclusive. No, there is something else holding women back. A pervasive, subconscious expectation that inexorably shapes female destinies.

Pervasive, Subconscious Expectations

That pervasive, subconscious expectation comes from the *Chaldee cancer* that has infected human society since the Fall. And it has practical, profound real-world effects. People's lives are being shaped by this discriminatory force and it is time to call it out. The disparity is greatest on the opposite extremes of the financial spectrum, both where poverty enslaves the "less fortunate" and at the top of the heap where leaders achieve the greatest financial success.

> *True justice for women will flow from true love, the kind of love that only flows from the heart of the Father.*

Of course, the *Chaldee cancer* cannot be eradicated by legislation. Legally imposed quotas and timetables have not produced gender equity. True justice for women will flow from true love, the kind of love that only flows from the heart of the Father. And this is why long term change will only come as the Kingdom takes root in the world.

Attitudes come from the heart, so making more laws or demanding employers give special privileges to females won't solve the problem. That only shifts the imbalance and foments resentment. And that's not to say that we don't need legislation that reaches for an ideal of true justice—just that we must understand that real change only comes from heart change.

If it's not a lack of legislation holding women back, and if it's not some shadowy, good ol' boys network, then what *is* holding women back? What keeps women consistently reaching for less than they could achieve? What keeps them limited in their expectations?

The answer? It's you and me.

We are still living daily within the framework of limited expectations handed down from generations gone by. The way we communicate with our spouses, with our children, with our co-workers, reveals those limitations. Starting at an early age, we train our children to fit within boxes created by cultural expectations.

From my observation—no doubt, there are exceptions!—little girls are not raised with the same expectations as little boys, especially if they are raised in a religious home. Moreover, the girls, if they want a career, are usually trained to believe that they must also manage the household. They must do *both* and do both well.

Mixed signals.

Think about the differing expectations placed on single moms versus single dads. Both single moms and single dads work outside the home and also manage the household, but single dads usually get a pass on *how well* it is done. A poorly kept house and ill-dressed children garners sympathy for the man: "He just needs a good woman to put everything in shape for him." The same mismanagement from a single mom would provoke sharp clucks of disapproval: "No wonder she can't get a man."

Expectations are different. *You know it's true.*

As I mentioned earlier, I grew up believing that as a woman I could do *anything*. But with that mindset also came the unspoken expectation that I should do *everything*. Can you see now how that mindset came to pass and how it has prevailed? Despite the advances in social justice, women carrying the domestic load in addition to other responsibilities is now part of our upgraded cultural psyche.

Here's the *Enjoli* jingle again:

> *I can bring home the bacon, fry up in a pan,*
> *and never let you forget you're a man*
> *Cause I'm a woman.*

That originally came from a 1962 song made famous by Peggy Lee. The idea was that to be a real woman meant you were supposed to take care of all the cooking and cleaning, take care of your man and your kids. Now we add work and making money to our schedule. The commercial advertised an "8-hour perfume for the 24-hour woman." You watch as the pretty, professional looking mom comes home from work and reads to the kids. She's both successful and sexy, and as a *reward* her husband surprises her by offering to cook for the kids that night.[14] It was assumed that would normally be her job too.

Thanks very much, Peggy Lee!

The prevailing idea was that women must do it all. If you got lucky, your partner might reward you with some help now and then. But a "real woman" should be able to handle it all. And I spent my life trying hard to measure up to that impossible standard, but I could never do it all well. Something always suffered.

Women are working harder than ever. Even with nifty labor-saving devices like washing machines, microwaves and dishwashers. However, many women are not reaching the top in either business or government, and it's not because they are not capable or because they are not allowed to do so. No, it's really more a matter of ingrained expectations. Women make choices along the way that cost them valuable opportunities.

Through general family attitudes and well-intentioned Sunday sermons, women are taught from an early age that they really aren't meant for leadership. Therefore, they should never aspire to it. We impose low-level expectations for our girls. The boys are also taught the same viewpoint, and they grow up alongside the girls reinforcing the expectations. The boys are conditioned to expect her service at home and in the

[14] To watch the commercial: https://www.youtube.com/watch?v=3N9K7eoVtm0

workplace. This undergirds the belief that she does not have equal potential at work.

In many churches the gender gap gets even wider. After all, doesn't God say women are supposed to be silent in the church? Doesn't He forbid them teach or have authority over men? The men feel vindicated by God himself.

Most families today cannot survive on one income. And, just like men, most women have dreams and visions that go beyond their family. However, women usually bear the responsibility to juggle both home and work, whereas most men merely "help out" at home.

Then there's the problem of single moms who are both breadwinner and homemaker. Today, nearly half of the children born in America will be raised in a single parent household. In 1980, a little more than eighteen percent of children were born to unmarried women. In 2008, that statistic is more than forty percent, nearing half of all children born.

According to the 2010 US Census, eighty-five percent of single-parent households are headed by women. Some of these are single parent homes due to death or divorce, but forty percent of all children born in the US right now are being born into homes where the father and mother were never married.

This is not just a "moral" issue, as some object. It's a preeminently practical problem as well. Single parent homes are having a profound effect on the wellbeing of our nation. For example, single parent homes are more likely to be gripped by poverty, which leads to generational, systemic poverty. In 2011, the Witherspoon Institute published an article, *"The Two-Biological-Parent Family and Economic Prosperity: What's Gone Wrong."*[15] This paper demonstrates the correlation between the decline of the U.S. economy and the rise of single parent households.

Tragically, the children of single parents often become the victims of the spirit of poverty with a full sixty-six percent living below the poverty line. Comparatively, only ten percent of children with two parents at home fall into that same category. "Since the rates of single-parenthood have risen so greatly, the largest proportion of the poor is no longer the elderly, but children."[16]

Much of this is driven by the idea that women were never meant to achieve at the same level as men. Girls have

> *It can be overwhelming when you think about how deeply entrenched the "women-were-created-to-serve-men" mindset is even today in the twenty-first century.*

been conditioned to believe that a man will provide for them. And when he does not, they are left out in the cold.

[15] Jeynes, William, *"The Two-Biological-Parent Family and Economic Prosperity: What's Gone Wrong":* http://www.thepublicdiscourse.com/2011/07/3532/

[16] *Ibid.*

Why is this still the case in our modern, progressive society? I personally believe it is the underlying religious beliefs about the role of men and women that are at the root of the issue. It is that cancerous *Chaldee* that has permeated every part of our society. It still exists in non-religious circles to be sure, although it is more discreet and subtle. However, in religious circles, this belief is often blatant and espoused as God's plan for humanity.

It can be overwhelming when you think about how deeply entrenched the "women-were-created-to-serve-men" mindset is even today in the twenty-first century. I would be deeply discouraged with the current statistics if I did not know for certain that God is personally, actively and strategically working to remove this cancer from His Body. We now hear greater numbers of Christian leaders all over America addressing the women's issue head on. They are confronting the status quo and raising the standards for women because God is on the message.

However, before we can see this cancer completely eradicated, there must be a clear and accurate diagnosis. Only after acknowledging that there is a genuine problem can treatment and healing begin.

That's what this series is all about.

CHAPTER 7

THE HEARTS OF MEN ARE NOW READY

After several years of struggling with what I thought was a discrepancy between God's heart and God's Word, the veil was finally being torn from my eyes. The "Why send Mary?" question led me to the "She has *Chaldee!*" dream, and that took me to the ancient Jewish documents written in Chaldee that had institutionalized misogyny in the Jewish traditions that so deeply shaped early Christian thinking.

Right in the middle of getting oriented mentally, spiritually and theologically to this new (to me) perspective on the women's issue, Holy Spirit dropped an exegetical bomb on me. And it was exegesis (digging out the meaning of a Scripture text) that I needed right now. I knew what God was saying to me, but I needed to understand the tough passages that seemed to restrict women so clearly and severely.

I needed a word on the Word.

One day, I sat in my study reading course content from Christian Leadership University. My heart was already wide open through the *Chaldee* dream to what God was planning to show me next. He was preparing to take me down into the biblical text like a submarine diving for the ocean floor. I knew that the root of religious misogyny was the *Chaldee* spirit in the Talmud, but I still needed to reconcile what He was showing me to what I could see plainly written on the page: "Let the women remain silent."

Still some serious cognitive dissonance.

I was never one to accept ideas blindly. I was hesitant to embrace other people's opinions. I've always wanted proof. But I could feel in my bones that Holy Spirit was about to lead me into clear teaching from somewhere that would resolve the interpretational conflicts I experienced. It felt like I was standing on the cusp.

Boy, was I right!

So, there I was, reading along in the course material, and I was introduced to an axis-tilting, planet-shaking book by Professor Joanne Krupp called *"Woman: God's Plan, Not Man's Tradition."*[1] In the book, Professor Krupp strode boldly up to the "let your women keep silent!" text and explained it without a stutter. She asseverated—which you can't do safely unless you're a professor—that Paul was *not* making that statement as an expression of *his* opinion; rather, Paul was quoting false Corinthian teachers. Indeed, the esteemed Professor went on, Paul *refuted* the chauvinistic position. Krupp argued without blinking that Paul's teaching actually says exactly the opposite of what we've all understood from the passage.

In our defense, it was an honest mistake. And in the next chapter, we will walk carefully through the text and explain our mistake in light of Professor Krupp's bold

---

[1] Krupp, Joanne, *Woman: God's Plan not Man's Tradition* (Salem, Oregon: Preparing the Way Publishers, 1999), 79-83.

asseveration. But just before we dive deep into the details, I need to recount one more incredible moment in my story. This word from the Lord actually gave me strength to pursue this revelation further, and it might help you as well.

Why, God?

When I saw what Paul was actually saying, I was completely undone. When I saw how wrong I had been —how wrong we *all* had been!—I was stunned. I sat silent, mouth agape, for a moment. Then, as the gravity and magnitude of what we had done throughout church history really started

> *How did we miss that? How could we have read Paul's word for millennia and not seen the truth before? How could we have believed the exact opposite of what Paul meant to convey?*

sinking in, a deep sense of horror gripped me.

Paul's words that had been so familiar to me for six long years now rang out from the page in a completely different tone. It was like I was hearing Paul's words for the first time. To be honest, when I read Paul's familiar words through a different filter, I cried and cried. I simply couldn't stop weeping as the reality set in.

Bawling like a baby may seem like an extreme reaction, but the truth that Paul had never meant to silence women overwhelmed my wracked emotions. How did we miss that? How could we have read Paul's word for millennia and not seen the truth before? How could we have believed the exact opposite of what Paul meant to convey? The *opposite!* When it was right there in black and white, staring us in the face all along.

Then my tears turned to anger. I sat frozen for a moment, breathing deeper, eyes narrowed, fists clenched. Through gritted teeth I finally gathered the composure to ask,

"Lord, for millennia men and women alike have believed that it was Your plan for women to be secondary. We thought it was Your will for women to restrict their voice and be submissive to the men. But God, if this was *not* Your plan, then why would You allow this to happen?"

It was a reasonable question, I thought.

I sat a while longer. Successive waves of reality kept washing over me. I would become still and then break out again in another spasm of weeping. It was surreal. The dark reality of where systemic misogyny had taken the human race kept sinking deeper and deeper in my awareness. It was both pervasive and malignant.

I cried out again,

"Lord! Women have been physically, emotionally and sexually abused, even enslaved, for thousands of years! And all of it flows from the insidious root of male superiority, which the Church has believed is Your perfect will for humanity. Father, if there is not at least a kernel of truth to this idea, then how could You have allowed Your precious Church to believe and institutionalize it? I don't understand."

I was really struggling.

Until this moment, I had believed that the hierarchical structure of men-over-women was God's original design that had been perverted by sinful humanity after the Fall. In other words, a restored creational structure would still use the "women-are-secondary-to-men" model, but in a good way. But now, my fundamental paradigm shifted: *God had never intended for men to be superior to women!* The hierarchical structure itself was a result of sin. It had never been a part of God's plan—not ever.

That made me mad. In fact, I became enraged when I realized that God's Kingdom economy never silences women or keeps them in a secondary position. The Fall did that. So then—and here's where my rage boiled over —why did God allow women to be placed in a subservient role if that was not His original intention?

Forgive me, but I had a moment. A long moment of wrestling with God. How could our good Father allow his daughters, the weaker sex, to suffer such abuses over the centuries, over millennia? The religious and political belief in a God-given hierarchical structure for men and women affected negatively every household that ever existed. If this was not God's intention for His people, then how could He let that happen? How could He let that happen and still be all-powerful? How could He let that happen and still be good?

There's the classic philosophical struggle: "If God is both good and great, then why does evil exist?"

The Hearts of Men Are Ready

As you might guess, God did not answer my accusation directly. But He did speak to me very clearly. And He said something that seemed a bit off topic for my overwrought soul:

"The hearts of men are now ready to receive the truth."

I had to think about that a minute. Embedded in that answer was a deeper answer about why God had not solved the problem before now. But all I could focus on at the moment was God's sonorous pronouncement: "The hearts of men are now ready."

Time stood still. I was alone in the heart of God, just the Triune God and me. And in His unexpected statement, I felt a surprising sense of peace—and a rising hope!—wash over me. The rage faded away. The tears dried up. In that moment, I still didn't understand why God permitted centuries of abuse. But I knew that the heart of God was profoundly grieved over the past and yet was ecstatically hopeful about the future: "The hearts of men are now ready!"

I could feel the leap of divine joy. Though I still had no answers for "why," yet I could understand fully, at once, that God did not want me to dwell on the past. I sensed on some level that dwelling on the past would forfeit the future, and the future suddenly looked bright.

Father God wanted me to be forward-thinking because the time was now right for Him to reveal His will and His plan. The time was right for Him to reveal the truth, for the hearts of men were now ready to receive the truth.

Astounding.

After centuries of male dominance, godly men around the world were humbling themselves under the mighty hand of God and were ready to courageously facilitate and fabricate a new world, a world of genuine equality between men and women. I knew it all at once, without argument or protest. This was a sovereign move of God, and I was meant to join it.

In order to join this move of God, I had to

> *Compassion restrains passion, which otherwise becomes zealotry apart from love.*

understand the heart of God. I was not ready to understand fully what Paul was teaching until God could uproot in me any potential resentment toward God, men and even other women. (Male-dominance-enabling women are usually the cruelest enforcers of patriarchy). When God refused to answer my questions about "why," He bypassed my outrage and pointed me to the ongoing divine transformation of the male heart. That simple, loving response inoculated me at once against any bitterness that could have poisoned my spirit.

Love, Not Vengeance

And that's why I am telling you this part of my story before we dig into the explanation of the first restrictive scripture passage. It is absolutely necessary that we align with the heart of Father God toward humanity before we attempt to understand theology. (Compassion restrains passion, which otherwise becomes zealotry apart from love.) As quoted above, Jesus is perfect theology, and He is the embodiment of love. Theology apart from love will simply rebound into opposite distortions of truth.

This is profoundly important when dealing with an issue rooted in such extreme injustice. As Bill Johnson also says, "A spirit of entitlement often hides within a cry for justice." As women, we can protest unfairness—and we should!—but without approaching the issue from God's heart of love toward sinners (particularly, in this case, male sinners), we will work out the correct theology and them promptly wield our now-rightly-divided scriptures as clubs to beat the brains out of men who oppose our newfound freedoms. And when that happens, the see-saw of injustice simply flips to the other side.

We see this so often. Feminists rightly struggle for female equality, but sometimes in the process get caught up in the same hateful spirit that drives misogyny. Some attempt to fight fire with fire: they return misandry for misogyny.[2] But as Martin Luther King, Jr. said, "Darkness cannot drive out darkness; only light can do that. Hate cannot drive out hate; only love can do that." And as Jesus said, "All those who take up the sword shall perish by the sword" (Matthew 26:52). Hatred kills the carrier. Acid destroys its container. As some say, bitterness is like drinking poison and hoping your enemy dies.

------

[2] Misandry is hatred for men.

Some feminists become obsessed with retribution. "We've got to get even! They owe us." But this inadvertently buys into yet another lie from the spirit of entitlement. Like James and John, mentioned earlier, women can align with the wrong spirit and not even know it. God is love, and when we operate out of vengeance, we break away from alignment with God. God's agenda is to break down the walls of hostility between men and women, and all other fragmented people groups, and to reunite us all in the recreated image of God revealed in His Son.

God is the ultimate feminist. But He also loves His sons, and He will not partner with hate whether masculine or feminine. Even when the hate has been provoked by centuries of oppression. It is not time for women to "get back a bit of their own." It is time for women to graciously forgive those who oppressed them and partner with the men whose hearts are now ready for new creation.

Sadly, many twenty-first century women, finally liberated from the chains of the past, feel they do not need men at all. Some even go so far as using sperm banks to have children rather than have men present in their lives. Some have swung the pendulum so far in the other direction that they become female supremacists, belittling men and viewing them as secondary to women. In their view, men are now nothing more than a condiment or side-dish, while they are the main course.

The see just saw-ed.

Listen to me closely, dear female friends. I feel your pain. I've been there, trust me. But Holy Spirit seized my heart that day to drive this point home: two wrongs never make a right. If you are a woman, please hear me. If we walk in entitlement, offense, bitterness, hostility or any form of female supremacy, we once again veer off the road of truth.

Some of the feminist writings I worked through did just that: they openly embraced female superiority. Their writing was sadly tinged throughout with overt hostility and unforgiveness. Not all of it, of course, but enough to make me draw back and evaluate the full spectrum of thought. I didn't want to drift from one ditch to the other. I wanted to love well, and hostility to men wasn't rooted in love. It was rooted in pain, and I wanted to heal that pain, not intensify it.

Precise and accurate theological information—in other words, interpreting Scripture exactly right—doesn't release love's astonishing power to effect lasting change. In fact, some of history's most infamous murders were done under the cover of "correct theology," the crucifixion of Jesus being the foremost. We can get all the texts interpreted just as Holy Spirit intended them, but if we do not interpret and apply them from a heart of love, then all our exegesis is in vain.

Let me assure you, the enemy does not care what ditch you are stuck in as long as you are stuck. Like Chuck. Satan does not care if you are a male supremacist or a female supremacist—he just wants you to be a supremacist of some sort, for then you are assured the fall that follows pride. The devil doesn't mind at all if you know the truth, as long as the lie of supremacy alloys its heart. The enemy just wants you bitter whatever it takes.

There is a better way. A way better than bitter. And that simple word, "the hearts of men are now ready," is the way forward to the better way. And readiness is what's been missing all along. Men and women *together* understanding God's heart for union and communion between the sexes as they *together* reveal the image of God. Only together can we reflect the image of the Godhead on the earth.

Male and female were made in God's likeness as a plural unity. God spoke the world into being, then formed us in His image with a creative, powerful voice. If we believe that women should be silent or kept separate, especially from influence and decision-making, then we have disfigured and defaced the image of God. The visage of God is marred in us when we are ripped apart. Only in union can we fully reveal the Triune God to the world.

> *If we believe that women should be silent or kept separate, especially from influence and decision-making, then we have disfigured and defaced the image of God.*

But here's hope: God is at work. He is moving upon the hearts of men and women across the globe to rise up and face this Chaldean giant. There's never been another time in human history when bigotry and discrimination are so widely condemned. How strategic is that?! God is moving.

The hearts of men and women are now ready for the revelation of this message. The world is ready. Even though many Christians have been taught that male supremacy is God's order, the truth will ring true to them. The Bride of Christ is ready for a revolution of thinking that will bring forth a revival of spiritual life. My husband, Gregory, likes to call it a "renaissance," a fresh, new move of God that fundamentally changes everything. Gregory does not see revival coming in small waves as it has so often in church history. Rather, he sees a major revival, with a surge of new life that brings forth creativity and touches every aspect of life—art, education, science, government, etc.

Let it be!

Father God interrupted my outrage for a reason. He wanted to make certain that I did not receive the truth without love. As Paul said, "Knowledge makes arrogant, but love edifies" (1 Corinthians 8:1). And that's why in this book series we are not rushing straight into the explanation of difficult texts. We must have a heart filled with love before we stuff our head full of knowledge. The message that will heal gender division is a message of love.

We must insist on approaching this topic with genuine humility. As I've heard Kris Vallotton say so often, the way forward is humility. The quest for equality cannot be powered by vengeance. It must be powered by love. And love seeks the unity of both male and female together in the image of God.

"The hearts of men are ready." Are the hearts of women ready? Are we ready to process the injustice we've experienced with true love and humility? If you, like me, feel a rush of fury when you consider the horrifying reality of female subjugation, then join me now in letting the hope of heaven transform our outrage into passion for change. Let's take the truth God is revealing and release healing into the world. The hearts of men are ready. The world is ready. Let's all get ready. It's time to unleash the Kingdom.

CHAPTER 8

REMOVING THE MUZZLE

N ow that I knew the hearts of men were ready, I was ready—ready for some serious theology. I needed answers. I was exhausted from being pulled back and forth, knowing in my gut that God did not approve of female subordination and yet not being able to explain the scriptures that seemingly prohibited women in leadership.

Now, Professor Krupp took me by the hand, so to speak, and led me back to 1 Corinthians 14. I was hesitant because I had worked through this passage so much, and as I mentioned before, each time I studied it, the restrictions just got worse. I was a little jumpy.

Yet I could feel a shift coming. It was as if Holy Spirit prodded me in the ribs and said, "Sit up, Susan. Answers are coming." I sat up. I could feel a change in my bones, and, boy, was I ever ready for it.

As I read Professor Krupp's take on 1 Corinthians 14, my heart quickened. I read it once, and then again. And again. This was exactly what I had been looking for: answers for Paul's writing that took him seriously as a Spirit-inspired writer of Scripture and did not simply find creative ways to explain it away. I leaned in.

Lean in with me.

The first step to understanding 1 Corinthians 14:34-35 is to read the context provided by the previous chapters. As they say, "A text without context is a pretext." Sounds right to me.

So here's the context.

To Put It All In Context

1 Corinthians 12-14 is all about unity. The discussion centers on how every Spirit-filled person—not just male persons—can participate in the assembly. Paul clearly communicates that *anyone* can share a song or a word. The emphasis is on *everybody* being able to participate. In 1 Corinthians 14, the text describes how no more than two or three should speak out or speak from the front. Paul explains that the meeting should be conducted in an orderly fashion so that it would not be chaotic with so many people involved.

> *When you assemble, each one has a psalm, has a teaching, has a revelation, has a tongue, has an interpretation. Let all things be done for edification. (1 Corinthians 14:26)*

The whole point *through* these chapters is that everybody has something to bring to the gathering—*everybody!*

The entire discussion is anchored by 1 Corinthians 13, the famous "Love Chapter." It is sandwiched in the middle of Paul's discussions in Chapters 12 and 14 of everyone having received gifts of the Spirit and how those gifts are utilized. The point, of course, is that the gifts of the Spirit operate from love.

The Love Chapter is a short but powerful description of how we should treat one another. It demonstrates how God, who is love, treats us. It shows us what love looks like in action:

> *Love is patient, love is kind and is not jealous; love does not brag and is not arrogant, does not act unbecomingly; it does not seek its own, is not provoked, does not take into account a wrong suffered, does not rejoice in unrighteousness, but rejoices with the truth; bears all things, believes all things, hopes all things, endures all things. (1 Corinthians 13:4–7)*

The Love Chapter drives home the point that it is not all about you. Or all about me. The gifts of the Spirit are given to the Church to build up the Church, not to promote certain high profile individuals. Paul makes it clear that spiritual gifts that do not operate from love are worthless. Again, love is the anchor.

But the nettle we must grasp for the purposes of our present discussion is that there are no gender distinctions set out in the Love Chapter. There's no, "Hey, all you guys! Love one another. Now, don't worry so much about loving the women—they are inferior creatures and won't mind being trod upon like doormats. Just be thankful each morning you're not one of those gals!" Not hardly.

In fact, there are no gender distinctions *at all* in 1 Corinthians 12-14 until we get to the infamous passage on shushing women. Through all Paul's teaching on the Body of Christ and how the gifts operate within the

Body, there is *not one single statement* that limits the function of the gifts by gender. In fact, as we shall discuss further later on, Paul specifically mentions women "praying and prophesying" in Church gatherings in Chapter 11. (1 Corinthians 11:5)

The point here is clear: throughout the flow of passages around the "prohibition verses," Paul assumes that women are included in all his teaching on spiritual gifts within the Church gatherings. As Paul lays out what "order" looks like in a Christian gathering, the rules of conduct have no gender distinctions.

For example, when Paul talks about honoring one another in love, he does not import Talmudic contempt for women. He does not suggest that we should show graded tiers of honor, the high ones for men and the low ones for women. Paul assumes that honor is unisex, gender neutral. Hierarchical honor is the antithesis of Paul's teaching in the Love Chapter.

Think about honor now, gentlemen. To a woman, it feels supremely hypocritical to open a door for her with a smug, "Ladies first!" but then ask her to take a back seat when it matters, when decisions of real import are made. Now, don't get me wrong: I appreciate it when my husband opens the door for me. I accept it as a gesture of honor. But, believe me, I would *not* feel honored if he ignored my opinion on matters of importance while ushering me gallantly through the door.

Those simple gestures of honor become valuable only in context. Someone who bows nobly before a king, but then dishonors him behind his back is a hypocrite.

For a woman struggling to overcome the gender barrier, a man opening a door for her can sometimes feel patronizing. She is perfectly capable of opening that door by herself.

However, when the Queen of England pulls up in that magnificent red Rolls, you will never see her hold up a hand in silent protest when the door is opened for her. She knows that the young footman is not insulting her capability. The young man is showing high honor. But the Queen can be confident in the honor showed to her because of the power she wields.

Honor without empowerment is patronizing. And that's why I appreciate it when Gregory opens a door: it is *real* honor, honor accompanied by real, shared power. Since my husband walks in honor toward me in every

> **Honor without empowerment is patronizing.**

aspect of life, I do not feel belittled when he reaches for the doorknob. Rather, I feel valued and respected.

And that's why the Love Chapter would be empty words for women if Paul really meant that selfless love was only meant to be shown among the men. No way. There are *no* gender distinctions hidden within the love of God.

As you likely know, the chapter divisions in our translations of the Bible were not in Paul's original letters. Chapters 12-14 are all continuing sections of one unbroken discussion. If you see this, then you will not miss the vital connection between love and honor that flows through the apostle's instructions.

All through these chapters, Paul instructs the Corinthians concerning spiritual gifts. He encourages believers to earnestly desire and pursue spiritual gifts, especially that *all* would prophesy. And the "all" here is not limited to "all men." Paul lays out guidelines for how *everyone* can function maturely in all of the gifts.

The underlying point is spiritual union for all believers. Spiritual gifts are given to build up the Body of Christ as one unified body. There is *no hint* here that Paul is promoting the exclusive union of male Christians. In Christ, there are no divisions between Jews and Gentiles, slaves and free, male and female, old and young, rich and poor, on and on. (See Galatians 3:28) The entire point of Paul's argument is that we are *all* one in Christ. Thus, the gifts of the Spirit are given to promote that unity.

In fact, if you read all of 1 Corinthians 1-16, the theme throughout is *unity*. To then abruptly stand up in the middle of this flow and shush half the Church seems out of sync with Paul's overall objective. It's out of context. Countless commentators have noticed the incongruity. It's like Paul turns on a dime. Total one-eighty. You hear that loud screeching sound? That's Paul jamming the brakes like a trucker jack-knifing an eighteen-wheeler going a hundred miles an hour. *It's not pretty.*

Shush the Women!

Here's the statement in full:

> *Women are to keep silent in the churches; for they are not permitted to speak, but are to subject themselves, just as the law also says. If they desire to learn anything, let them ask their own husbands at home, for it is improper for a woman to speak in church. (1 Corinthians 14:34-35)*

Talk about incongruity on steroids.

It simply doesn't fit. Of course, if Paul actually said it, then we would just have to accept it, incongruity notwithstanding. That's what we've done for years. But Paul didn't say it, as we shall see in a moment.

There's no mitigating the harshness of the statement. Countless commentators have tried to no avail. As I told you earlier, when I tried to interpret it to match what I felt God saying in my gut, it simply didn't work. This is a profoundly harsh instruction.

For example, the Greek word for "improper" here actually means "shameful" or "disgraceful." So, literally, verse thirty-four says that it is "disgraceful" for a woman to speak in church. And as I pointed out before, the full sense of the command is that a woman should "make no sound" in church. Nary a whisper.

Most traditional evangelical churches try to brush away the actual command here and rephrase it as merely a "limitation on female leadership," a limitation that is subjectively defined based on the cultural milieu of the local Church. I've heard brilliant teachers of the Word attempt this with something like:

"Well, Paul really did not mean total silence, of course. He just simply meant that women should be limited within whatever cultural setting they serve."

(How the women are limited, of course, the men get to determine.)

But that's not what the text says at all, is it? It plainly says that it is a *"disgrace"* for women to utter a sound in Church. Discerning what the text plainly says is not the difficulty in this passage; the difficulty is in obeying it.

These same teachers who will not accept what the text plainly says will then use these verses to insist that women must be submissive to the men in the church and cannot teach. And they will do so while claiming that they *must* do so in order to be faithful to the text. They solemnly affirm that they don't want to, of course, but they simply have no choice because *"the Bible tells me so."* But what the Bible actually tells them, that women must not utter a sound in Church, they refuse to teach. It's rather sad to thump your chest about how faithful you are to unpopular scriptures while *disobeying the exact scriptures you claim to obey!*

Trying to use a verse that forbids a woman uttering speech at all as a basis for teaching that women are simply limited in leadership is an exegetical nightmare. You cannot allow women to sing in choir and teach kids but then use this "total silence" passage to only restrict women from teaching adult men. It is intellectually and theologically dishonest. You don't need a Doctor of Divinity to know you cannot interpret and apply Scripture that way.

Again, "countless commentators" keep popping up trying to soften the blow and make the passage less anti-women. But it is no use trying. The verses are explicit: women are not permitted to make a peep in Church. Even if their name is Little Bo. (Sorry, couldn't resist a little comic relief.)

Best efforts aside, "let your women keep silence" means no women singing in the choir. No women giving announcements. No women teaching children in the nursery. Women are not allowed to engage in any activity that requires speaking.

I have never seen a church like that. In fact, in my experience, there are always more women participating in church than men, and naturally, they all talk. Are we violating this scripture by letting women use their vocal cords when we assemble? If this is Paul's admonition to the Church, then yes we are.

But I have yet to see *one* church anywhere, not even the most traditional, forbid women to make any sound. Why not? Is it because these churches find it impractical to enforce? No, that's exactly what the Jews did in Jesus' day: the women were required to be absolutely silent. So it can be done.

Surely we would all enforce this command as well no matter how impractical if we actually believed that absolute silence for women was God's will. Yet in our heart we cannot accept that. We know instinctively that such an extreme ban is not right. No one in evangelical Christianity honestly believes that women should not speak in church. That's why we massage the text to make it say less than it does. The fact that we must finesse the interpretation to avoid what it plainly commands is our first clue that something is seriously wrong.

It gets worse.

What Does the Law Say?

Paul adds that women should "subject themselves, just as the law also says."

> **There is not one example of God commanding women to "subject themselves" to men. "The law" simply doesn't say that.**

Here's another red flag. Bright red. Such a command for women "to subject themselves" cannot be found in the Law anywhere. There is no such commandment in the Pentateuch[1] or anywhere in the Old Testament. The only verse that even comes close is Genesis 3:16: "He shall rule over you." But this statement is God describing what the curse upon humanity will be like, not God describing things as they should be—*description*, not *prescription*. And this curse is exactly what Jesus came to break. (Galatians 3:13) I seriously doubt that Paul would seek to reimpose what Jesus came to destroy.

---

[1] The Pentateuch is the first five books of the Bible, also called "The Law."

We do see plenty of cases in the Old Testament where wicked men "subjected" women, but God never approved. In fact, the Law of Moses codified fair treatment for women in several instances where pagan culture was terribly abusive. There is not one example of God commanding women to "subject themselves" to men. "The law" simply doesn't say that.

Something's fishy here.

If the Law of Moses is not the reference here, then to what "law" is the quote referring? There's really only two good possibilities, as I see it. First, "the law" could be Roman law, which legislated and codified male supremacy in various ways. In most pagan cultures, anti-female sentiment was deeply engrained. Maybe that's "the law" that required women to "subject themselves"? Maybe.

Second, "the law" could refer to the Jewish Traditions of the Fathers that had been elevated over the Law of Moses. The Oral Law that was later written down and codified as the Talmud was called *Halakha*," defined as "the collective body of Jewish religious laws derived from the written and Oral Torah."[2]

Now, that makes sense. As I mentioned earlier, the first century Church was deeply impacted by its Jewish roots. The entire New Testament is the record of the ongoing struggle for the Church to emerge from Judaism into the ekklesia of King Jesus. Every book in the New Testament is wound around this thorny issue. Check out

2 https://en.wikipedia.org/wiki/Halakha

Galatians, Colossians and Hebrews for the clearest examples. But it is everywhere.

"The law," then, is likely a reference to Rabbinic Law, which as we've seen was shockingly anti-women. Among the Jews of Jesus' day, misogyny was woven into culture and upheld legally. It was the "law of the land." And if this reference is to the Rabbinic Law, then—I'll be danged!—there's that *Chaldee* spirit again. (You do remember that the earliest form of the Talmud was written down in Chaldee? Good.) Though there's no way to be sure, all that Holy Spirit said to me about "she has *Chaldee!*" certainly makes me lean that way. This passage certainly manifests the *Chaldee* spirit.

Regardless which "law" Paul has in mind, he was *not* quoting Scripture to reinforce female subjugation. Paul knew the Law of Moses like the back of his hand, and he would never have misquoted the Law like that. And that's important when proving beyond doubt that Paul did not require women to be silent in Church. As we will see in a moment, the command to be silent and the validation of "the law" were not Paul's words at all.

Ask Your Husband

The next verse, "If they desire to learn anything, let them ask their own husbands at home," also makes no sense as an expression of Paul's sentiment. The early Church, starting with the ministry of Jesus, welcomed women to be active "learners" within the Christian community. The story of Mary choosing "the good part" by sitting at the feet of Rabbi Jesus to learn is an earthshaking, culture-realigning story. (Luke 10:38-42) Jesus taught with the "question-and-answer" method of the rabbis, which means that Mary's inclusion in the class would have allowed her to ask questions.[3] And the assumption would also have been that students in a rabbinic school were learning to teach others. Why else would they learn?

Jesus' invitation for women to gather with His disciples and learn was a total break from Jewish tradition where the women were expressly forbidden to participate in Torah studies. In fact, Rabbi Eliezer ben Hyrcanus declared at the close of the first century, "Anyone who teaches his daughter Torah teaches her lewdness."[4] Rabbi Eliezer also wrote, "Women's wisdom is solely in the spindle." He then added, with particular venom, "The words of the Torah should be burned rather than entrusted to women."

Other rabbis of the same period were less restrictive. Some taught that women could attend Torah instruction as silent learners, but only to "listen, not to study."[5] Rabbi Gamaliel, Paul's mentor, encouraged greater equality for women (which further strengthens the argument that Paul would not ban women from

---

[3] *See* Matthew 13:36 and Matthew 15:15 for examples of the private, discussion-based instruction that Rabbi Jesus' disciples enjoyed. This is the sort of discussion that Mary was invited to share.

[4] https://jwa.org/encyclopedia/article/torah-study

[5] *Ibid.*

engaged, inquisitive learning).[6] But Rabbi Eliezer's total ban on teaching women became the controlling mindset within Judaism until the nineteenth century. There's no doubt that the ban wrongly attributed to Paul on women learning interactively would have reflected the mindset of the Judaizers of the first century.

But not Paul. Paul was insistent that men and women are equal in Christ. Remember the *context*: the early Christian format for worship was fairly informal: gather around the table for prayer, communion, fellowship and teaching. (Acts 2:42, 46) Look at who is gathered around the table: men and women, slaves and free, Jews and Gentiles, sharing the bread and wine,

> *The Church welcomed women to the table where the Word was taught and discussed. It would have been odd to enjoin silence upon the women even when discussion around the table was such a central part of "having church."*

listening to the teaching of the apostles, asking questions, praying together, singing together, encouraging one another, doing life together, sharing *koinonia* together.

Women are at the table. Sitting right there beside the men. Unlike the Synagogue, the Church welcomed

---

[6] Philip B. Payne, *Man and Woman, One In Christ* (Grand Rapids: Zondervan, 2009), 35-37.

women to the table where the Word was taught and discussed. It would have been odd to enjoin silence upon the women even when discussion around the table was such a central part of "having church."

Think about how awkward Paul's prayer meetings in Philippi would have been if he banned women speaking. Lydia, Paul's first European convert, was the leader. In fact, many of the early Christian gatherings were hosted by women. Female hunger for truth was a powerful engine for early Church growth. It doesn't seem likely that these truth-seeking women were required to ask questions only after arriving back home to their husbands.

What about Priscilla and Aquila, the ones who "explained the way of God more perfectly" for Apollos? (Acts 18:26) Can you imagine Paul shushing Priscilla and telling her save her questions for Aquila when she got home? I don't think so.

New Glasses

Something's up here. There's more going on than meets the eye. Have you ever seen the movie *National Treasure* with Nicolas Cage? In the movie, there was a secret treasure map that could only be seen with a special pair of glasses. It was hidden in plain sight. You could be staring right at the paper but not see the map without those glasses.

That's exactly what this text is like. The answer is hidden in plain sight, but we need special interpretive glasses to see it. In verse thirty-six, Paul hands us new glasses.

Let's read the full quote again in context:

Let two or three prophets speak, and let the others pass judgment. But if a revelation is made to another who is seated, the first one must keep silent. For you can all prophesy one by one, so that all may learn and all may be exhorted; and the spirits of prophets are subject to prophets; for God is not a God of confusion but of peace, as in all the churches of the saints.

The women are to keep silent in the churches; for they are not permitted to speak, but are to subject themselves, just as the Law also says. If they desire to learn anything, let them ask their own husbands at home; for it is improper for a woman to speak in church.

Was it from you that the word of God first went forth? Or has it come to you only?

If anyone thinks he is a prophet or spiritual, let him recognize that the things which I write to you are the Lord's commandment. But if anyone does not recognize this, he is not recognized.

Therefore, my brethren, desire earnestly to prophesy, and do not forbid to speak in tongues. But all things must be done properly and in an orderly manner. (1 Corinthians 14:29–40)

Get this: you *all* may prophesy. You *all* may learn. You *all* may be exhorted.

But then,

> *The women are to keep silent in the churches; for they are not permitted to speak, but are to subject themselves, just as the Law also says. If they desire to learn anything, let them ask their own husbands at home; for it is improper for a woman to speak in church.*

"All" may prophesy, learn and be exhorted. "All" the men, that is...

Really? The same Paul who declared that men and women are equal in Christ? The same Paul who included women in his ministry and recognized them as equals with male ministers? (Romans 16) This same Paul then cancels half the Church and bans them from participating? It just doesn't flow. Verses

> **There's a reason for all the abrupt shifts in thought: Paul was quoting an idea that was not his.**

thirty-four and thirty-five just seem to abruptly yank the steering wheel to the far right. It doesn't align with Paul's thought.

Apparently, Paul agreed. Because he yanks the wheel back the other way, back to unity, equality and inclusion. Verse thirty-six is the key:

> *Was it from you that the word of God first went forth? Or has it come to you only? (1 Corinthians 14:36)*

Now, those are interesting, out-of-nowhere questions. As we've noted, the brash command to "silence your women!" was a herky-jerky one-eighty all by itself. Add these abrupt questions, and we're all suffering from exegetical whiplash. It simply doesn't fit.

There's a reason for all the abrupt shifts in thought: Paul was quoting an idea that was not his. Let me prove it.

Disjunctive Participles and Other Hidden Treasures

Look back at the context. Chapter after chapter, Paul weaves in the underlying theme of unity between all believers. There's no exception made for females. Everyone who is filled with the Spirit—and that includes "your sons and daughters" (Acts 2:17-18)—is gifted by the Spirit to build up the body. And all this is done by everyone through love.

Then, abruptly: "Tell all the women—the same women who are filled with the Holy Spirit, the same women who pray and prophesy—to be silent and subject themselves to the men." Then, tires squealing, passengers screaming, Paul whips back the other way: "Who do you think you are?! Did the message come only from you, big shot?! Or are you, smarty pants, the only one to hear the Good News?!" I mean, in the interest of full disclosure, I added a few salty phrases in there for the fun of it. But this is definitely Paul's tone.

Check your nearest commentary and see if others see what I see. It's an awkward flow, to say the least.

(1) Everyone is filled with the Spirit and gifted to build up the church.

(2) Everyone except women, that is. They must be silent and subject to men.

(3) Cause you're not the only one who hears God's voice!

See how weird that is? I'm telling you, there's something else going on. The key to "what's going on" lies in the Greek text, the original language in which Paul wrote this letter. Although many translations ignore it, verse thirty-six actually begins with a disjunctive participle in the Greek. (All you grammar nerds will love this!) "Disjunctive" simply means "to disjoin from, or oppose, what was just stated."

The dictionary defines the grammatical use of the disjunctive this way, "Syntactically setting two or more expressions in opposition to each other."[7] So, verse thirty-six starts with contradiction—a rebuke!—of what was previously stated. That's why it feels so abrupt: it's "disjunctive."

The disjunctive participle in verse thirty-six looks like a single letter, the letter "ἤ" in Greek. In English, scholars transliterate it like this: "ē."

Author and theologian Gilbert Bilezikian says,

Recent scholarship has called attention to the disjunctive force of the participle "ē" that introduces verse thirty-six. It has the impact of an emphatic repudiation of what precedes it. A colloquial equivalent

7 https://www.dictionary.com/browse/disjunctive?s=t

such as "nonsense!" would come close to rendering the break between the prohibition statement (vv. 33-35) and Paul's response to it in verse thirty-six.[8]

Did you get that? That tiny little participle, which is often overlooked, has the effect of a strong disapproval of what was previously stated. Although many translations ignore it altogether, the King James Version translates it, "What?" Verse thirty-six should start with a negative exclamation. Maybe even a "what the heck?!"

The Revised Standard Version does a better job of presenting the impact of Paul's response in verse thirty-six:

> *What! Did the word of God originate with you, or are you the only one it has reached? (1 Corinthians 14:36 RSV)*

> **These words of exclusion are not Paul's words. Paul is quoting the Corinthians.**

Paul is not confirming the exclusion of women just quoted in verses thirty-four and thirty-five. No, indeed. He is contradicting it. He is shouting, "Nonsense!" to the idea that women must remain silent and subject as "the law," most likely the rabbinic law, demanded.

---

[8] Gilbert Bilezikian, *Beyond Sex Roles: What the Bible Says About a Woman's Place in Church and Family*, Third Edition (Grand Rapids, MI: Baker Academic, 2006), 115.

All of this suggests what I've been pointing toward all along: *these words of exclusion are not Paul's words. Paul is quoting the Corinthians.* Let me prove it some more.

Rhetorical Method: Questions & Answers

The entire letter we call "1 Corinthians" is Paul's response to a series of questions that the Corinthian church had sent to him by letter. This is evident from 1 Corinthians 7:1:

> *Now concerning the things about which you wrote. (1 Corinthians 7:1)*

In Chapter 7, the questions are about celibacy. In Chapters 8-10, the questions answered are all about eating food sacrificed to idols. In Chapter 11, Paul answers questions about head coverings and communion. In Chapters 12-14, it's all about spiritual gifts. In Chapter 15, Paul answers their questions about the resurrection.

The entire book is structured as answers to questions. Moreover, Paul writes the letter using a didactic tool called the "rhetorical method."[9] He employs a diatribal discussion technique that was common in Paul's day both among Jews and Greeks. The most famous version of diatribal teaching is the Socratic Method, but Jewish rabbinic teaching employed various

---

[9] For a powerful presentation of this idea, see Lucy Peppiatt, *Women and Worship at Corinth: Paul's Rhetorical Arguments in 1 Corinthians* (Eugene, OR: Cascade/Wipf and Stock, 2015).

forms of the question-and-answer approach. Jesus uses this rabbinic, rhetorical form in Matthew 16 when He tests the disciples' understanding of who He was.

> *Now when Jesus came into the district of Caesarea Philippi, He was asking His disciples,*
>
> *"Who do people say that the Son of Man is?"*
>
> *And they said, "Some say John the Baptist; and others, Elijah; but still others, Jeremiah, or one of the prophets."*
>
> *He said to them, "But who do you say that I am?"*
>
> *Simon Peter answered, "You are the Christ, the Son of the living God."*
>
> *And Jesus said to him, "Blessed are you, Simon Barjona, because flesh and blood did not reveal this to you, but My Father who is in heaven.* (Matthew 16:13–17)

Here, Jesus teaches with questions: "Whom do people say I am?" Then, "Who do you say that I am?" The questions provide the framework for the lesson. Paul also used this method in Romans, though his interlocutor in Romans is imaginary, as far as we know.

> *Therefore you have no excuse, everyone of you who passes judgment, for in that which you judge another, you condemn yourself; for you who judge practice the same things. And we know that the judgment of God rightly falls upon those who practice such things.*

But do you suppose this, O man, when you pass judgment on those who practice such things and do the same yourself, that you will escape the judgment of God? Or do you think lightly of the riches of His kindness and tolerance and patience, not knowing that the kindness of God leads you to repentance?

But because of your stubbornness and unrepentant heart you are storing up wrath for yourself in the day of wrath and revelation of the righteous judgment of God, who will render to each person according to his deeds. (Romans 2:1–6)

Dialogue, whether real or imagined, was a prominent feature of first century teaching among Jewish rabbis and Greek philosophers. However, Paul's rhetorical method doesn't always make it obvious where the questions are. In other words, Paul weaves the words of others into his responses without always making it clear that he's quoting. Scholars have worked carefully through 1 Corinthians to identify the quotes, but it's not always clear.

For example, look at 1 Corinthians 7 and you'll see a more obvious example of the rhetorical method. Look first at the NASB rendering, which has no quotation marks to show the question. Then look at the ESV where the translators inserted quotation marks to show the question:

Now concerning the things about which you wrote, it is good for a man not to touch a woman. But because of immoralities, each man is to have his own wife, and each woman is to have her own husband. (1 Corinthians 7:1–2)

No quotation marks here. But then, the ESV with quotation marks:

Now concerning the matters about which you wrote: "It is good for a man not to have sexual relations with a woman." But because of the temptation to sexual immorality, each man should have his own wife and each woman her own husband. (1 Corinthians 7:1–2)

The ESV and other versions add the quotation marks to highlight what translators have learned over the years: Paul often quotes without making it obvious. And of course the original Greek of the New Testament had no punctuation marks as we do in modern English, which means that subtle textual clues, context, logical flow and consistency within the argument are all translators have to go on.

Yet learning to recognize those subtle indicators can often make the quotes obvious once we see them. For example, the "but" at the first of 1 Corinthians 7:2 signals Paul's objection to the quoted statement. Paul is *not* saying that "it is good for a man not to have sexual relations with a woman." In fact, he will say exactly the opposite:

But because of the temptation to sexual immorality, each man should have his own wife and each woman her own husband. The husband should give to his wife her conjugal rights, and likewise the wife to her husband. For the wife does not have authority over her own body, but the husband does. Likewise the husband does not have authority over his own body, but the wife does.

Do not deprive one another, except perhaps by agreement for a limited time, that you may devote yourselves to prayer; but then come together again, so that Satan may not tempt you because of your lack of self-control. (1 Corinthians 7:2–5)

The Corinthians were proposing—most likely due to Paul's example as a single apostle (v. 7)—that celibacy was more "spiritual" and preferred for Christians. Paul shoots that down right away. Yes, celibacy *can* be the right choice for some believers, but *only* if Holy Spirit calls and gifts a person for that specific assignment. Paul does not support

> **Both the husband and wife have authority over the other. Does anyone here see how crazy that statement was in a first century context?**

the statement: "It is good for a man not to have sexual relations with a woman." And the "but" in verse two makes that clear.

While we're here, by the way, we should not skate past one of the most provocative, revolutionary statements in the Bible regarding women. While answering their questions on celibacy, Paul says,

For the wife does not have authority over her own body, but the husband does. Likewise the

husband does not have authority over his own body, but the wife does.

Both the husband and wife have authority over the other. Does anyone here see how crazy that statement was in a first century context? In the first century Roman Empire, the woman had little, if any, rights. The entire system was built around the exclusive, total rights of men.

The first half of the quote could have come from the mouth of any Greek, Jewish or Roman teacher of that era. They all believed that "the wife does not have authority over her own body, but the husband does." Every man in the synagogue, or in the Roman Forum, would have jumped up to shout, "Amen!" at that. But the second half—"likewise the husband does not have authority over his own body, but the wife does"—would have left them dumbfounded, shell-shocked, speechless with dismay.

What did he just say? Zeus, have mercy! Did he just say what I thought he said?!

The men of Paul's day would have freaked out. And they probably did. That's most likely why Paul had to overthrow their attempts to silence women. They, as men have done since the Fall, were keen to preserve their prerogatives of power.

Paul's message here is mutuality. We will talk more about mutuality in Book 3. But I just don't want you to miss it here in 1 Corinthians 7. It was radical and revolutionary.

But our larger point for now is that Paul frames his argument as a question-and-answer dialogue throughout 1 Corinthians. Quote a Corinthian question and respond. It's all through the letter. Scholars largely agree on the following examples: 1 Corinthians 1:12; 3:4; 6:12–13; 7:1; 8:1, 4, 8; and 10:23—and possibly also 4:6b; 8:5a; 12:3; 15:12, 35.[10] A growing number of scholars also recognize 14:34–35, the main text under review, as another example. And, as we shall see in Book 3, 1 Corinthians 11 is most likely the most extensive example of Paul's rhetorical method. Scholars also agree that Paul's quotes are not always signaled with overt written cues.

The point to grasp now is that it should not be surprising to encounter an interjected question right in the middle of 1 Corinthians 14. It's exactly how Paul wrote throughout the entire letter. This is important to clarify lest someone object that we are just twisting the text just to produce the desired interpretation. We're not. Understanding the rhetorical method actually clarifies Paul's teaching and prevents skeptics from rejecting Paul's biblical authority on the grounds that he was inconsistent and untrustworthy.

The rhetorical method actually explains why Paul, who argued so forcefully for female equality elsewhere, would suddenly inject apparent misogyny in the text. It's pretty hard to explain how Paul could show such honor

---

[10] Again, see Lucy Peppiatt, *Women and Worship at Corinth: Paul's Rhetorical Arguments in 1 Corinthians,* (Eugene, OR: Cascade/Wipf and Stock, 2015)

to women like Priscilla and Phoebe and then suddenly tell them, "Shush, now! Women are not allowed to speak. It's a disgrace, Priscilla, for you to talk when the church gathers. Phoebe, I know you're a deacon at Cenchrea, but you must never say one single word while the church is gathered. That would be *shameful!*"

We'll talk more later on about Paul's inclusion of women in his ministry, but we must now reckon briefly with the inconsistency. If Paul actually told women to be silent—just after telling them in 1 Corinthians 11 that they could pray and prophesy!—then he was a literary schizophrenic. Paul was too thorough, too meticulous for that. But taking the rhetorical method into account unifies the text and explains clearly what Paul was saying.

Sum It All Up

Think about what we've seen so far:

- In 1 Corinthians 11:5, Paul discusses women praying and prophesying. In 14:34-35, he bans it. Was the man schizo? I don't think so.

- The statement banning women quotes "the law" as its basis. As we've seen, this most likely refers to the Rabbinic Law, which Paul would have been violently opposed to using as a guide for Christian practice. There's no way the same man who wrote, "You who are seeking to be justified by law; you have fallen from grace" (Galatians 5:4), is going to impose "the law" out of the blue like this. No way.

• Immediately after the statement barring women from speaking, Paul exclaims, "What?!" and proceeds to skewer their presumption.

All this makes it clear that verses thirty-four and thirty-five are simply not Paul's words. He seizes a statement that *the Corinthians* made and overthrows it violently in one passionate exclamation: *"Nonsense!"*

So let's read it again, in context with what we've learned:

> For you can all prophesy one by one, so that all may learn and all may be exhorted; and the spirits of prophets are subject to prophets; for God is not a God of confusion but of peace, as in all the churches of the saints. (Vs. 31-33)

Everyone—and that includes females!—can prophesy as long as it is done in order. Then Paul quotes a portion of the letter to him from the Corinthians, which they would have recognized immediately:

> The women are to keep silent in the churches; for they are not permitted to speak, but are to subject themselves, just as the Law also says. If they desire to learn anything, let them ask their own husbands at home; for it is improper for a woman to speak in church. (Vs. 34-35)

Paul responds to this statement with outrage, as he was wont to do:

> Nonsense! Was it from you that the word of God first went forth? Or has it come to you only? (V. 35, disjunctive participle included)

Paul then drives the point home with an appeal to his apostolic authority:

> *If anyone thinks he is a prophet or spiritual, let him recognize that the things which I write to you are the Lord's commandment. But if anyone does not recognize this, he is not recognized. (Vs. 37-38)*

Herein lies a clue to who it was among the Corinthians that was trying to silence the women: it was most likely an "anyone" (or several "anyones") who "thinks he is a prophet or spiritual" and was setting himself up as the authority over church polity and practice. Paul yanked his (or their) chain by declaring, "Let him recognize that the things which I write to you are the Lord's commandment."

> **The most astonishing thing about all this is that Paul was not silencing women—he was silencing those who would silence women!**

Paul had already addressed the factions warring for supremacy in Corinth (1 Corinthians 1:10-13), and there is no doubt that certain leaders were trying to impose their will on everyone. It seems evident to me that the attempt to silence the women was just another power play by the men jockeying for position. They wanted the authority to determine who was "recognized," and appealed to the Talmudic "law" to support their claims, which indicates that the men were influenced by Judaism (maybe the "Cephas party"? — 1

Corinthians 1:12). Paul flips it around: "But if anyone does not recognize this, *he* is not recognized."

Everything in 1 Corinthians is about unity through love. And the demand that the women be "shushed" is neither unity nor love. It simply does not express Paul's sentiments.

And finally, Paul wraps it all up:

> *Therefore, my brethren, desire earnestly to prophesy, and do not forbid to speak in tongues. But all things must be done properly and in an orderly manner. (Vs. 39–40)*

The most astonishing thing about all this is that Paul was not silencing women—he was silencing those who would silence women! Paul removed the muzzle. And yet, here we are two thousand years later still arguing about whether women can lead. The word given by Paul to liberate women has been flipped around and used to subject them.

Father God never intended for His daughters to be silenced. The sheer arrogance of the men at Corinth to think that they had the authority to determine who was "recognized," who had the right to take the floor. The immortal gall that they would shush the Holy Spirit because He dared speak through a woman. And yet, the heirs of these false teachers shush us still. God is grieved.

No wonder I wept.

CONCLUSION

HONOR

One of the most powerful things I've learned on this journey is the importance of honor. We will talk more about honor in Book 2. But I want to close this opening volume with a healthy dose of honor for the men and women who have brought us this far.

Honor and the Kingdom

It is easy to highlight all that's still wrong with the world, but the truth is, I would not be allowed to highlight anything if it had not been for pioneering men and women who fought tirelessly for female freedom. My freedom to advocate for more freedom was purchased at a high price by those who've gone before me.

I also want to honor those who struggle with the limitations placed on women but feel conflicted by what appears to be "the clear teaching of Scripture" banning women in leadership. There are so many still today who are pushing back against the relentless tide of male dominance unleashed like a tsunami upon the world. I admire the honest attempt made by so many pastors to release women into leadership and ministry in spite of generations of Christian tradition. So many have done so while struggling as I did with how to balance the heart of God toward women and the seemingly harsh passages restricting them. My prayer is that the explanation of 1 Corinthians 14 (and others passages we will consider in this series) helps. Paul was not restricting women. He was in fact restricting the men who sought to limit women. What an ironic twist!

Thankfully, there are many female–friendly churches today. Many choose not to deal directly with the prohibitory verses because they appear so anti-female. They just avert their eyes and keep moving along. All they need is the revelation that Paul was not silencing the women. Rather, the venerable apostle was rebuking those who wanted to silence half the Church. Paul wasn't having it then, and we shouldn't have it now.

Many leaders know instinctively that God would never want women silenced, but they don't understand what Paul was actually saying. They believe he must have been limiting women to some degree here—the teaching seems so plain. The question is how much?

Each church or group of churches answers that question differently. To varying degrees, churches allow women to have a voice, to teach and lead. So, limitations are imposed because it seems unfaithful to do otherwise. In these female-friendly organizations, women are freer than in the more traditional ones, but limitations still exist.

Some try to explain away Paul's prohibitions against women by saying they were only culturally relevant to his day—meaning women had to be silent back then, but they do not have to now. Some get imaginative and propose that the women in Corinth were unusually immature. The women (so the story goes) were being loud and disruptive, shouting out questions to their husbands from across the assembly. That sort of thing would never do, so Paul gently encouraged the women to save their questions for later when they could "ask their husbands at home."

As we've seen, that interpretation doesn't work for several reasons, but I understand the impulse to mitigate the brutal force of the actual command. Paul did not say here, "Now, dear sister in Christ, if you don't mind, it would help us all maintain decorum if you'd hold off shouting your questions across the Church. If you can, beloved woman of God, please speak quietly. There's a good girl!" No, that's not at all what the quote said. It said, to put it as harshly in English as it is in the Greek, "All you women, sit down and shut up!"

> *In nearly every modern church, there are still some type of gender-based restrictions because of the false belief that the Scriptures require them.*

The churches and denominations that strive to empower women still struggle with where to draw the line. That's understandable. They believe there *must* be a boundary for women somewhere because of these prohibitory scriptures. They don't feel comfortable simply editing the Scriptures out. So, in their quest to empower women and still honor the Word, they set the bar as high as they feel comfortable.

Depending on the church or denomination you visit, there is a huge difference in where the bar is set. Yet, in nearly every modern church, there are still some type of gender-based restrictions because of the false belief that the Scriptures require them.

Some churches allow women to hold every office in the church except that of elder. (1 Timothy 3:1-13, explored in Book 3) Others may allow female elders, but they purposely choose women who will think in total alignment with established male leadership. Sort of like a newly liberated "yes-woman." They fear that females in general would not be able to handle conflict with the men. They also fear that adding women to the leadership structure would bring too much change too quickly. So female elder selections are based on how well the women can fit into the current male-dominated structure.

This practice defeats the very purpose of having women join the leadership team in the first place. To fully reflect God's image in the boardroom, both masculine and feminine voices are necessary. One is not better than the other, even if it is different than yours.

In other churches, the female leadership restriction line is drawn way up near the very top. In these churches, a woman may be an associate pastor or elder, but she may not hold the most senior leadership position. Perhaps if she is married to the senior leader, then she can be a co-leader, for her husband would still be above her. However, a woman cannot hold the top position. That role is reserved for a male.

The strangest limit I've seen is where a woman can be the senior pastor as long as she has a husband at home to whom she is submitted, or as long as she has some form of male covering.

But here's the point I'm making: all of these guidelines, no matter how they're structured, are based on some level on these misunderstood verses in 1 Corinthians 14 and a few other passages we will cover later on. The same verses that Paul used to overthrow latent misogyny within the Church are now used to reinforce it. All these various forms of female restrictions stand in direct violation to what Paul actually taught.

The traditional position seems absurd to people outside the church. In a world where women lead as CEO's of billion-dollar corporations, Prime Ministers and Presidents, the Church seems archaic. It's hard to understand why a woman may be trusted with a Fortune 500 corporation but not a 50-person congregation. Makes no sense.

Such thinking seems utterly ridiculous unless you sincerely believe that these female gender restrictions are God's will. If the traditional interpretation of these verses was indeed God's divine order, then it would make perfect sense that church leadership would have an *obligation* to discriminate against women. The Church does not govern its affairs according to worldly values.

However, most church leaders today are torn. Most know that discrimination and lack of freedom is contrary to God's love. So they are confused, pulled between

Paul's words and God's heart. Most pastors and leaders I know want to champion women and lift them up. Thankfully, the fresh understanding of Paul's teaching recounted above reconciles these discrepancies and liberates these leaders to liberate women. With a proper interpretation of Scripture, pastors are empowered to follow God's heart without violating His Word.

My sincere prayer is that what we've studied above has made it clear now that any limitation based on the "women are to keep silent" passage is *not* the will of God. God never placed a muzzle over the mouth of His daughters.

The idea of any gender-based restriction is a lie intentionally planted by the enemy to subvert and disempower the Church as a whole.

> *Imagine how much prayer and prophecy, decree and declaration, leading and loving has been silenced by silencing women in the Church.*

Imagine how much prayer and prophecy, decree and declaration, leading and loving has been silenced by silencing women in the Church. Paul never meant to silence or limit women. In fact, his purpose in these verses was to do the exact opposite. The ones Paul meant to silence were the men trying to silence women.

The Gospel of the Kingdom

You would think that the next step on my journey would have been to work carefully through the rest of the texts that were understood to prohibit women in leadership. Now that Holy Spirit had opened my eyes to what Paul was actually saying in the 1 Corinthians 14, "shush your women!" passage, I was eager to start working afresh through 1 Timothy 2 and 3, Ephesians 5 and the Genesis 2 and 3 creation texts that supposedly demonstrated that God ordained the subjection of women. Now that I had seen how badly we misunderstood 1 Corinthians 14, I was ready to tackle the remaining passages. And, of course, I did work through them some. But the fuller understanding of those passages would come later after Holy Spirit drew me aside for a five-year Kingdom detour along a scenic route that turned out not to be a detour at all. *The Kingdom was the destination!*

All along the way, Holy Spirit had led me carefully with powerful, guiding words that carried me through layers of understanding. The "Why send Mary?" question got me started; the "She has Chaldee!" dream carried me further; and "The hearts of men are now ready" word finished the first cycle of transformation in my thinking.

I was now fully convinced that the Church had been infected with the Chaldee cancer and that it was time to be healed. What I didn't expect was that Holy Spirit would take me first into a deeper understanding of the Kingdom of God and show me how the women's issue was fully intertwined with the gospel of the Kingdom.

At first, when Holy Spirit started drawing me into Kingdom studies, I didn't see the connection. What does the Kingdom of God have to do with women in leadership? Well, *everything,* that's all. What I found out is that the Kingdom of God releases a totally different view of power and how humans relate to each other. I learned that male supremacy comes from another kingdom, the kingdom of darkness, and that the Kingdom of God could never sustain the chauvinist system that had oppressed women for so long. It simply could not produce such oppression.

I also learned that correct theology could be as destructive as wrong theology if it is driven by the wrong spirit. Maybe more so. The root of the gender wars is a struggle for power, and the gospel of the Kingdom totally reorients the human lust for power. And winning the fight over Scripture could perversely become another power struggle. Just getting the correct interpretation of Scripture would not "lay the ax at the root of the tree," as it were. Only the Kingdom's radical reorganization of the human heart and human society could do that.

I learned that rushing headlong into proof texts and authoritative sources, that waving the Bible over my head and gesticulating wildly in valid protest, would only *increase* the conflict between men and women, not end it. Marshaling arguments and winning debates would not bring shalom. Only the peace of Christ released through the Kingdom could do that. I discovered that learning the "truth" about women detached from the gospel of the Kingdom could degenerate into petty triumphalism. Only by undermining the competitive structures of human society and overthrowing hierarchicalism through the gospel of the Kingdom could real rapprochement between men and women be achieved.

This is why Jesus came preaching the gospel of the Kingdom long before He explained the intricacies of doctrine to His disciples. The gospel of the Kingdom is the foundation for all truth.

The next few years became a whirlwind adventure into understanding the gospel of the Kingdom. You see, the Kingdom was the essential piece to seeing how men and women fit together in God's purpose. And that's exactly what I want to do with this book series. If you are like me, you are eager to get to the other prohibition texts and dismantle the religious structures of male (or female) supremacy once and for all. And we will. But first things first. Holy Spirit taught me that the gospel of the Kingdom must be—absolutely *must* be!—the foundation of our understanding. Otherwise, the pendulum swings and male supremacy gets replaced with female supremacy.

And that's what we will do in Book 2 of this series: we will take a wide excursus through Kingdom theology. The gospel of the Kingdom is not extraneous to the women's issue; it lies directly at the heart. Don't skip it! Holy Spirit certainly wouldn't let me skip it, and I soon found out why: misunderstanding the role of women in the Church prevents the gospel of the Kingdom from fully taking root in the world. I am not exaggerating for effect when I say that the Kingdom cannot come in the world as long as half its agents—the female ones!—are immobilized by false power structures carried over from the world into the Church. The *Chaldee* cancer must be surgically removed.

It has now taken me two decades to put the puzzle pieces together. You see, that day in my study, I did not have a grid for understanding God's Kingdom. My thinking did not line up with His thinking at all. I was a very devout Christian, and I had become well acquainted with the Bible, but I had no clue about His Kingdom. I began to realize that King Jesus recruited us to be kings and priests in His Kingdom here on earth, but I did not even know what being a king in God's Kingdom was supposed to look like.

> **King Jesus recruited us to be kings and priests in His Kingdom here on earth.**

Does that sound odd? Maybe. But I think it's true for many Christians. For most of us, our understanding of the Kingdom is elementary. Like most Sunday School trained believers, I thought God's Kingdom was far away in a distant place called "Heaven." (Sort of like "in a galaxy far, far away...") I thought the Kingdom would come when Jesus returned in a far-off place and time. I just believed what I had been taught and some of what I had received by theological osmosis.

What I did *not* know is that the Kingdom of God came to earth in the incarnation of Jesus, then came to dwell within you and me through the outpouring of the Holy Spirit and will finally come into the world all around us as we are salt and light in the world.

I did not know that the Kingdom is God's will being done on earth, right here, right now. Jesus came to establish the Kingdom here among us. Think about it, now: when Jesus came preaching, He did not preach "the gospel of salvation" (though His gospel certainly includes salvation). Rather, Jesus came preaching "the gospel of the Kingdom."

The message of the Kingdom is everywhere in Jesus' preaching. Everywhere Jesus went, He talked about the "Kingdom." His parables often began with "the Kingdom is like..." There were times when Jesus healed someone and then declared, "The Kingdom has come upon you." (Matthew 12:28; see also Luke 10:8-11) Jesus saw healing as evidence that the reign of God was manifesting upon the earth. Amazing!

This was Jesus' pattern everywhere He went. If you take only *The Gospel of Matthew* as an example, it seems like every page Jesus is talking about "the Kingdom of Heaven," which is Matthew's unique idiom for "the Kingdom of God." Here's the simple reality: Jesus taught more about the Kingdom than anything else.

Before I could fully understand the significance of the women's issue apart from my own wrestling with an impossible call, the call to preach God's word in a Church where it was *verboten*—before I could see the Big Picture of why it mattered cosmically, globally, universally and not just personally—I had to learn about *the unity of men and women within the Kingdom.*

That meant I needed more understanding on the Kingdom. Thus the additional five-year journey.

Without proper Kingdom context for the women's issue, I was destined to fail miserably. This would be especially true if I convinced women that the Church and the world got it wrong all along and successfully empowered women to lead without understanding the Kingdom. Yes, the girls would lead as God intended, but lead to *where?* What good is it to lead if we are leading people astray?

No, we needed more than just correct theology on the women's issue. We needed a revelation of the Gospel of the Kingdom so empowered women would be empowered for the right reason and to lead in the right direction. That's where we're headed next in Book 2.

EQUIPPING PEOPLE TO UNLEASH THE KINGDOM.

Gregory & Susan Dewbrew founded *Kingdom Brewing* to develop resources for equipping people to unleash the Kingdom of God in every realm of life —family, church, business and culture —until we see a new Kingdom renaissance. If you are passionate about seeing the Kingdom take root in every nation, then join the renaissance. It's the adventure of a lifetime! Learn more at **kingdombrewing.com**.

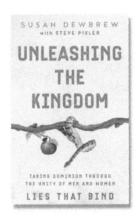

READ ALL THREE BOOKS IN THE SERIES!
AVAILABLE AT **KINGDOMBREWING.COM** OR AT YOUR FAVORITE BOOKSELLERS.

MORE RESOURCES FROM KINGDOM BREWING

Want to go deeper? Sign up today for
UNLEASHING THE KINGDOM ONLINE COURSE at
kingdombrewing.com.

Want daily encouragement? Sign up for the **DAILY VITAMIN** with Gregory Dewbrew at
kingdombrewing.com.

Steve & Jeana Pixler live happily ever after in Mansfield, TX with their six lively children. Steve & Jeana, with an amazing team of Kingdom influencers, lead Freedom Life Church in Mansfield, TX.

To learn more about Steve & Jeana and to discover more Kingdom resources available from their ministry, visit **stevepixler.com**.

NOTES

NOTES

NOTES

CPSIA information can be obtained
at www.ICGtesting.com
Printed in the USA
LVHW030313140821
695160LV00010B/899

9 781737 221609